Soul of American Warriors

By

Elizabeth Kilbride

I

Cover design by Matt Johnson

Cover Photo credit USMC and Elizabeth Kilbride

The author, Elizabeth Kilbride, can be contacted at:

myladyindc@msn.com

First printing, Oct. 2009
© November, 2007 Elizabeth Kilbride
Printed in the United States. All rights reserved.

ISBN: 978-0-9824982-6-2

Father's Press, LLC
Lee's Summit, MO
(816) 600-6288
www.fatherspress.com
E-Mail: fatherspress@yahoo.com

Acknowledgments

It is impossible for me to name all the wonderful people who helped by providing me with advice and guidance in preparing to enter into a war zone. All the encouragement you gave me helped pave the way and contributed to the completion of this book.

A special thank you goes to the following individuals, because without you, this journey would have only been a dream: Lt. Col. Francis Piccoli, I pray you never regret having asked me the question that started me on this journey. Bill Ervin thanks for giving me the honor to join you and your fellow veterans in Vietnam. John Strasburg for your unwavering friendship. Allen Larson, you were right, this experience changed me forever. Jeff Luce and Chuck Westbrook, you are the best. Colonels Mike Greer, Bill Sinnott and Mike Nunnally, Lt. Gen. James Mattis, MGen. Bob Hollingsworth, MGen. John Sattler, General Peter Pace, Mr. H. Ross Perot, Daniel Smith (the best Country Music Singer in Nashville), Diane Castle (Wachovia Bank, NC), David Ritz (Ritz Camera), Rosetta Stone Company, KwikPoint, Brigade Quartermaster, All the members of VFW Post 1822 of Plymouth Massachusetts. Capt. Miguel Alvarez and Sgt. Jim Griffin (The best Public Affairs Liaison's a writer could have in a combat zone). Matt Johnson for creating an amazing book cover. Leann Johnson and her Dad the Rev. William H. McMichael, for all your prayers and especially those prayer clothes you sent me. To the wives, siblings and children of those who serve in uniform, thank you for your thoughts, suggestions - You truly are the lifeblood of the military and our country.

Lt. John D. Borrero, MSGT Bivens, Lt. Colonel Matt Jones, Sgt. Major Lloyd Hatfield, Major Kasner, Lt. Jake Sandmeyer, Lt. Pryor, Lt. Col. Don Caporale, and the 4th & 6th Civil Affairs Team of Korean Village. Col. Link Crowe, thank you for paving the way! Linda and Paul McAlduff for giving me a quiet place to reflect and write. Larry Hampton, I love ya Bro! Tony O'Brien, thank you for covering my six. All my friends who supported me throughout this project and to Donna Westbrook for the countless hours of editing that helped me make this book a final product, thank you.

To all the Vietnam and Iraqi Veterans who gave me their time, shared their stories and unwavering support, it was an honor to have spent time with you. Those in the Maryland National Guard, Navy Seabees and Marine Air Wing, thank you for helping to make my experience in Iraq a memorable and safe journey.

Marian Inslee, thank you for allowing me to remember Ray in such a special way.

Mike and Father's Press, God Bless you for believing in this book.

Last but not least a special acknowledgement to all those in 3LAR, thank you for allowing me to spend time with you in the desert; I will never forget how you taught me to survive with very little!

To my Muse: I thank you for being with me on this journey. Without you, I would have had a very different experience. I will never forget your being there for me when I needed you the most.

Dedication

To my brother Jack, I Love You
Now I understand

And

Raymond Inslee
Sgt. United States Army
A Company, 1st Battalion, 503rd Infantry
Killed in Action: 29 March 1970

*A Special Tribute in memory of those
members of the*
*United States Marine Corps, 3LAR Battalion
who gave the ultimate sacrifice for Freedom*

Cpl Phillip E. Baucus
Killed in Action 07/29/06

LCpl Anthony E. Butterfield
Killed in Action 07/29/06

Sgt Christian Williams
Killed in Action 07/29/06

PFC Jason Hanson
Killed in Action 07/29/06

Cpl Adam A. Galvez
Killed in Action 08/21/06

HN Chadwick T. Kenyon
Killed in Action 08/20/06

LCpl Randy Lee Newman
Killed in Action 08/21/06

LCpl Shane P. Harris
Killed in Action 09/03/06

Always Faithful,

I will never forget you!

Author's Personal Message

Trust is a great responsibility. In a combat zone, trust among those around you helps to keep one another alive. A breach of that trust often results in loss of life.

When a non-military person travels to a combat zone, they must earn the trust of those around them. Fortunately, for me, I earned the trust of those I encountered in Iraq, which afforded me greater access to observe their daily life.

To travel with such brave warriors without restrictions is a gift. A gift that can never be returned, except by not divulging information that might put them, civilians and coalition forces in harm's way.

Prologue

When one thinks of our Armed Forces they think of military personnel whose main purpose is to kill, what we do not always realize is they are more than just a uniform and a weapon.

My journey into Iraq afforded me the opportunity, as an embedded writer, to experience life in a combat zone, along side brave warriors. It started out with one single objective in mind; to observe the *"Compassion of an American Warrior,"*© but along the way something happened - I saw more than just compassion. I witnessed the pure passion and dedication of our warriors, helping the people of Iraq rebuild their lives and give them the freedom all humans deserve. I was not only proud to witness their actions, but also humbled as an American.

One will never see their passion and dedication in Hollywood's typical movies or even on television, because it would reveal who they really are: humanitarians, builders, and stewards of the land.

Without having time to absorb what was experienced in Iraq, I immediately embarked on another journey, a journey to Vietnam with a group of Vietnam Veterans. The pieces of the puzzle began to come together and I now understood the price that will be paid in the future.

Upon returning home and having time to unwind, I was besieged with guilt as I tried to sleep in a safe, comfortable bed, take a shower, or even open my own refrigerator. All the while, thinking of our warriors sleeping in the desert, battle-damaged buildings, on uncomfortable cots, enduring shower tents, (if they had one at all), eating in institutionalized chow halls or eating those nasty MREs (Meals Ready to Eat). How typical it is for Americans to take for granted the bounties, safety and freedoms so absolutely void of existence in many regions of the globe.

This is when I realized, something happened to me while I was in Iraq, something far beyond my comprehension and understanding. A twist of fate turned the Compassion of an American Warrior into the story you are about to read. Like the pieces of a puzzle coming together for the first time, a very powerful defining moment revealed a new understanding. Life, as I knew it, changed forever in that instant.

CHAPTER 1
DEFINING MOMENT

In everyone's life there is one defining moment that brings everything in your life into perspective. When that moment happens, it is like a slap upside the head, a wake up call so to speak, and you begin to see things as they really are. Psychologists call these "significant emotional events." You might be wondering what this is like. The only way I can explain it is it's like your favorite novel being transformed into a movie. You see the characters come alive and they interact with each other for the first time. You begin to see each character for who they really are and realize that each character is an individual. As the story unfolds, you begin to understand and see how each character has their own agenda, and how that agenda drives them throughout the storyline. You sympathize with one or two because they touched a cord within your soul, instead of seeing them for who they really are. When you finally decide whom you are going to cheer for, the story twists and you become confused because you never saw it coming until the story ends. During those last few final moments you still believe the characters you were supporting were what you "thought they were", only to realize that the characters you were supporting the entire time were not who they appeared to be at all. They were much more dangerous than you ever thought.

When you take each character of your movie and transform them into real issues, you begin to see how each is affecting the world around you. This is when your defining moment happens - reality kicks in and a new screen flashes before your very eyes. It's as if the show of your life has just been stopped, rewound, and fast-forwarded. You begin to see the pieces falling into place. While you watch as this new movie flashes before your eyes, you begin to see a different side of the story and you can see things as they really are in life. 'The Plot' is thicker than you ever thought it was. The storyline you thought you were absorbing was not the storyline at all, instead it is much more dangerous than it ever was on the surface. Just then, the fantasy world into which you escape suddenly shatters before your very eyes.

You try hard to absorb this new information while trying to comprehend and make sense of it all. This is when you begin to make changes in your own life. This is the beginning stage of your defining moment! You take a few steps back and begin to analyze your life. As you try to put things into perspective, you slow down and take a moment to smell the roses. You notice things you never thought to notice before in your hurried life; the big picture before you. You also come to realize that the characters in the story created a deception and you become very angry. This is when you ask yourself one question: Are you willing to do anything about it, or are you going to move on in life without ever affecting a change? This is the true essence of your defining moment - what do you do about it?

Upon returning home from Iraq in April of 2006, there would be a culmination of many powerful defining moments for me – moments of clarity. Like anyone else who has ever returned home from a combat zone, one begins to see things in life differently. Your eyes are now wide open and you begin to see things as they really are. In my own life, I began to see old friends and associates differently. People who I once helped achieve their ultimate goals in life of becoming an elected representative; I now realized had succumbed to selling their souls and integrity to the sharks on Capitol Hill. Lobbyists whom I socialized with over the years and considered friends, I now saw as the shallow individuals they truly were. I became disgusted at the loss of perspective and values I once held.

Listening to the rhetoric on the news, I became sick as I watched those same friends from Capitol Hill on varied news programs and talk shows, spouting off the propaganda their political party thrust upon them to say. I watched their eyes and remembered conversations about the dishonesty of our elected officials and their promises never to impeach their integrity, character, or morals; yet they themselves now believed every word coming out of their mouth. I also remembered their promise of never turning their back on those who helped them to achieve their goals; yet, their promise was discarded once the oath of office was taken. It should have been my first clue of their succumbing to the shark-infested waters of public life, of public office.

This is when I made the choice; my defining moment would not be stored upon a shelf, only to be thrown out as trash when I die. It was time to take a stand and effect a change. Why would I bare my life to the public eye like this? It is quite simple really - many who come to Washington, DC never have their voices heard. It is not because they cannot speak, but because they do not know how to break down the barriers for their voices to be heard. I know how to break down these barriers and for that reason, I decided to lend my voice to those silent voices throughout the country you will never hear from – the brave men and women who serve in our Armed Forces. These American's chose to be in the military. They stepped up to the plate and took an unselfish oath to defend and protect against foreign and domestic enemies who attack the very essence of freedom. It is for them I write this book. This story, my story, intertwines with their story, and has my entire life.

Knowledge

"If a nation expects to be ignorant and free in a state of civilization, it expects what never was and never will be... if we are to guard against ignorance and remain free; it is the responsibility of every American to be informed." Thomas Jefferson

I love the words of our founding fathers. Whenever I am lost for the beginning of an article, or speech, I go back to the founding fathers for inspiration. Many of their words resonate true in our time, possibly even more than they did in their day. The above passage is more important today because of our world climate.

One has to wonder why I would bring up this quote. Many have asked why anyone would want to enter into a combat zone if they were not in uniform, or paid big bucks by a contractor. It is simple – if you do not know or understand something, you have a responsibility to educate yourself. I believe in education as the founding fathers did, and I wanted to see with my own eyes if what was being portrayed on the news was the whole story. If left up to the media, you will never get the full truth of any story. You will only receive what they want you to hear. When the opportunity arose to go to Iraq, I jumped at it.

If any American believes it is easy to enter a combat zone, then they are gravely mistaken. If for some reason they think the process of preparing oneself to enter a life such as this is so easy, I challenge them to try it, then come back and tell me if I am mistaken. Those who think it is pieces of cake, to prepare and enter a combat zone are ignorant of what reality is in the lives of our military personnel. I would suggest they seriously remove those rose-colored glasses. These are the doubting Thomases of this country. They who fear to make the choice to join the ranks of the honorable and serve our country to defend and protect – these are the ones who we should fear the most. It takes a very special person to love a country so much and believe in freedom so deeply that they would be willing to stand before God and Country and take the oath to protect and defend – an oath that might cost them their lives. They are the true heroes of our country. Unless you are willing to take off those rose-colored glasses our society forces us to wear each day - you will never see the leaders, builders, healers, and stewards of the land who make up the United States Armed Forces – they are so much more than just a uniform and a weapon.

CHAPTER 2
HUMBLE BEGINNINGS OF A WRITER

Memories of the past are like a beacon, flickering in the night to help us find our way out of the dark. Some are brighter then others, reminding us of the joyous days in our lives. Others seem to be blips or fragmented light representing memories we would rather forget all together. I wish I could say it was hard for me to bring up the darker memories of my past, but I cannot. These are the memories, which until recently, I did not realize were the driving force in life. They are memories, which allowed me to feel emotions such as fear, anxiety, stress and loss for the first time in my life.

I have been told that under ordinary circumstances these kinds of feelings would hinder a person from being productive. In many cases, others who lived a similar life, to the one I did growing up, allowed these feelings to hinder them and their future. Yet in my case, they had such an impact on my life, it put me on a different path altogether. A path I would not understand until after I had taken this journey. A path that would never allow me to forget those who gave the ultimate sacrifice for the freedoms I hold dear. This path also created a love and passion for those in our Armed Forces who sacrifice every day so that we might be free to do as we wish in our daily lives. They are the men and women who make me proud to be an American. Thanks to them, I have a new understanding of their struggles. Now they have helped me understand things from my childhood, and put to rest a few ghosts who have haunted me for a very long time.

My story begins with my association with two men who left home as proud Americans to serve in uniform; they were sent to a place called Vietnam – Jack Kilbride and Ray Inslee. The first was my older brother and the other a family friend who I always considered one of my 'other brothers' while growing up.

Since my childhood, I have struggled to understand why Jack, who went off to war, came home to a society that never considered him a hero. This struggle has caused me a great deal of pain over the years, because to me he has and always will be my hero. Like my father before him, who fought in two wars and many military related situations before I was born, my brother was no different. They both felt the passion for the United States of America in their hearts when they took the oath to protect and defend as they entered into the United States Military. To this day, that oath taken by every service member is taken seriously. An oath that is part of the American heritage and a legacy we should all hold dear. Yet, many Americans feel the oath is not worthy of being respected. I, as an American, as the daughter of a World War II and Korean Veteran, and most importantly as the sister of a Vietnam Veteran, feel it is worthy of my respect. The men who took the oath during the Vietnam War and every other war or conflict this country has been involved in deserve respect and admiration for their service to our country.

Over the years, I have encountered many veterans of the Vietnam War and have learned so many things from them. The information was like pieces of a puzzle I felt I could never solve. Perhaps it was because I never served in uniform that I could not understand how to solve the puzzle. On the other hand, maybe it was because the full story was never revealed. To combat veterans, these are the stories, which should never be revealed to a female. I was determined to solve that mystery one day.

I have been asked many times why I decided to take this journey. I did not have to ponder the question because it was a journey long over due. It started when I was a child growing up in Levittown, New York, the first planned community for veterans.

Levittown was the kind of community one left the major cities of New York for, in order to raise their children and give them a better life. It was a family town, filled with soldiers, sailors, Airmen and Marine veterans of two wars, World War II and Korea. As the first community in the country dedicated to those returning from World War II, it became an influence and new trend in the home building industry - track style homes began to spring up in Pennsylvania, Florida and Puerto Rico with the same name. Every home was sold to those returning from the war. These homes were affordable to those who served our country proudly. From Cape Cods to Ranch style homes, the homes were made of sturdy construction. Community pools, markets and hardware stores were conveniently located throughout each section. Each home cost between three and six thousand dollars for those returning heroes, to raise a family in the suburbs of Long Island.

Hence, these heroes influenced the humble beginnings of my life. Therefore, I had many surrogate fathers, uncles, and cousins to encourage in me the core values of America, to help nurture my love of our military and our country. They were the men who shared their tales of war, helping me to understand the struggles and sacrifices it took to safeguard a nation while upholding the legacy I was born into. A legacy filled with honor, dignity and the sacrifice of those who went before us, from the Founding Fathers to the heroes of today. These men gave me the love of Country, Duty, and Honor I hold dear today. They gave me an overwhelming sense of pride for those who heard the call of Country, Duty and Honor and joined the United States Military to carry on this legacy for future generations.

By the time I came along, my Dad had long since retired from the United States Army as a Major. He'd seen more battle than he cared to acknowledge. My mother was at home, taking care of the house and my siblings while dad was in Europe, Korea, and God knows where else he was sent during his military career.

For me, my fondest memories are those of hanging out with Dad and his friends at the local VFW Post 9592, the American Legion, and Knights of Columbus Halls. I remember sipping my cola and nibbling on slim-jims as he and other veterans told stories of their military careers. I can still recall listening with fascination to the Pearl Harbor Veterans recalling the horror of that infamous day back in 1941. How the country united behind them as they went to war. Then to hear the soldiers who were at the Battle of the Bulge recalling how cold it was during their days in Europe, while those who served in the Pacific described the heat, the humidity and the blistering sun. Still others discussed their war, in Korea. All the while, my father rarely spoke of his service, except to correct someone on their facts as the alcohol took over their memories. He never did this with disrespect, but with a gentle probe to refresh their memory, so they were not thought a fool. My experiences with the men of those previous wars gave me a sense of their sacrifice and a deeper admiration for those who choose to put on a uniform every day. I can only smile as I remember impassioned discussions over which branch was better than the other, playful bantering with bright smiles, as they teased each other over their beers and cigarettes. I will never forget the picnics, barbeques, smokers and those parades on Memorial Day and Veterans Day. These were the days of my childhood. To this day, I cannot walk into a VFW Post without remembering these beautiful memories, especially if there is a smell of stale air from cigarettes and beer. Each time I enter into one of these halls of heroes, I have the overwhelming feeling of coming home.

CHAPTER 3
MEMORIES OF THE PAST LONG FORGOTTEN

When I began to write this book, I also began to remember the darker memories that were buried deep within my soul. These were the memories associated with pain, fear and worry. Any child who has a sibling or parent fighting in a combat zone, experiences new found feelings of fear, anxiety and stress other children never feel. They are feelings that cannot be helped, no matter who you are. However, in my case, when you are the daughter of a career officer, these feelings were never to be shown. Therefore, I suppressed these feelings and went on with life. It was easy for me; I had no idea how to react any other way, except to be strong. It would not be until later in life that I would begin to fathom their intensity or understand how they helped shape my life for years to come.

While I began to look back on my childhood, I realized there were things I could remember as if they happened yesterday, while others were fragmented. As we get older, some memories from our childhood begin to fade away, while others stand out like beacons from a lighthouse, illuminating memories that form who we are today. These are the memories we will never forget over time. Some will say it was the day President Kennedy was shot and killed, or when the first astronaut walked on the moon. While these historical moments still stand out in my mind, as if they happened yesterday, a few others stood out even more because they were personal memories and touched my heart.

As a child growing up in the sixties one would think I would have memories of peace marches, anti-war protests and flower children, but for some reason I do not remember any of those things. The only memories I can recall were worry, fear, anxiety and yes, loss. I was all of about four years old and I can remember clearly sitting on the sofa folding laundry with my mother, watching her daily shows when the screen of our black and white television changed and my mother began to cry. I watched the television and heard some strange man talking about something I did not understand. They showed pictures of people crying, screaming and police running all over the place. She abruptly got up, ran to the phone, and dialed a number. Then I heard her say, "Johnny, they have killed the President." I watched in silent confusion as the man on the screen said, "President Kennedy had been killed by Lee Harvey Oswald in a place called Dallas Texas'. We sat in silence as they showed a plane with a flag draped box being lowered from its belly. Even as a young child, I felt the horror of this situation, even though I did not understand what death or murder was at the time. My siblings would tease me for the next few years because for some reason I remembered, even at a young age, the specifics of the President was killed.

Many things happened in the next few years that I cannot recall, but I can clearly remember one fateful day in our kitchen. I was standing at the foot of the stairs by the front door at the entrance to the kitchen. My father was sitting in his usual spot at the kitchen table when the back door opened. In walked my brother Jack and his friend Bobby. They stood at the sink, behind my mother who sat at the table too. My father looked up and they began to speak. I do not remember the words clearly enough to write them, but I do clearly remember the horrified look on my parents faces. My Father did not speak for a few minutes and my mother held his hand atop the table. Then I heard a word I had never heard before, "Marines." Both Jack and Bobby were smiling, but the look on my mother's face was not a smile at all, it was silent horror. My father stood and gestured for the boys to join him outside. My mother slowly dropped her face into her hands and began to cry. It was a look, I never wanted to see again, but I would see it many times over in the coming years. I was so young at the time I had no idea what was really happening.

What seemed to be years to a young child was only a few months later, I stood on the front lawn and watched two men walking up the street towards me. They were tall and confident, never wavering in their steps, and they walked with such determination. As they crossed the street, the taller one smiled and walked past me, ruffling my hair before entering the house. It was Jack! He was no longer the boy who went off to camp - he was now a United States Marine.

It would not be long after his leaving that another memory, would be forever burned into my memory. Still vivid to this day, I remember watching my mother cry as she made dinner each night. Meanwhile, Dad muttered under his breath as he watched the nightly news. Any mention of Hill 881 would haunt my father for days. I would not understand the meaning of those tears or the muttering until many years later, when I too would experience the same feelings they once felt, when someone I loved went off to war.

Three other distinct memories came into focus as I began to write. The first was when my father gathered us all together before Jack came home on leave from Vietnam. For some reason I remember his facial expression and his words very clearly. He had a look of both guilt and worry on his face as he stood smoking his cigarette, telling us that Jack would be home shortly. I was so excited; my big brother was coming home. Once he began to speak, my excitement diminished quickly. His main request was to not ask questions when he returned home. I remember him saying that Jack had just been through hell and was not going to want to talk about his experiences, nor would he want to dwell on it. The year was 1968 and Jack was returning home on leave after being in Khe Sanh, during something called the Tet Offensive. I did not understand what my father meant at the time, but I respected his wishes and stayed clear of Jack upon his return home. This was something I now regret doing.

My second memory was of just before the holidays in 1969. The kitchen door opened and a man wearing an Army Uniform walked in. His beautiful eyes sparkled as he stood, smiling from ear to ear, and saluted my father. My father stood, stoic and returned his salute. Laughter broke out between the men as my father shook the soldiers' hand, and then gripped his father's hand. I, on the other hand, stood quietly behind my father, my heart pounding in my chest with pure excitement as I gazed upon this gorgeous man in uniform. There standing beside my father was the first man I had ever had a crush on, Raymond Inslee. Ray and his dad stopped by to say hello before he was to return to his unit, the 173rd Airborne Brigade, and then he was off to a place called Vietnam.

Ray was a handsome man, but in his uniform, he was a beautiful sight to see. While both our fathers chatted, Ray came over to say his good-byes, promising to write. I giggled, as any young girl would do at the age of eleven when an older, handsome man even spoke to her. Before he left, he handed me a wallet-sized picture of him in uniform. I looked down at the picture and about fainted. He was so handsome in his uniform, those beautiful blue eyes and the smile I loved so much, now in the palm of my hands, to see forever. Then he gave me a big hug and said he would come by to see me when he returned, but I had to promise to be a sweet angel while he was gone and not an evil little girl. We both laughed at the reference and of course, I promised to be good. After saying goodbye to my father, he and his dad left. I remember running to the front window, beaming from ear to ear as I watched them walk out to the car, all the while giggling to myself, I was going to marry that man one day. My father just laughed at me and smiled. [Evil little Girl Reference: Ray would always pick on me when we were at the VFW during family gatherings and would call me an evil little girl. This was because I was always teasing the boys around me. Only he could get away with teasing me, because any attention I got from him was worth it and I loved every minute of it.]

The worst memory I have was of one particular day in March 1970. My father and I had just returned from the bakery, we'd picked up fresh rolls, bread and Danish, as we had done for as long as I could remember. We were sitting at the kitchen table eating breakfast when the phone rang. Dad answered it as he always had, but this time his face became drawn and his eyes glazed over as he listened intently. When he hung up the phone, he looked over at me without saying a word. Tears began to well up in his eyes, but he never said a word to me. On impulse, he reached for the phone and dialed a number. He uttered a few words then hung up. He stood up and stared at me for a second then went to grab his hat. My mother came in the room and he told her what had happened. "Ray has been killed. I am on my way over to the house to be with the family." Hearing his words, my heart sank deep in my chest and I began to cry uncontrollably. For the first time, my father showed emotions by hugging me and reassuring me, everything was going to be ok. I begged him to allow me to come with him. I remember him saying that if I came with him, I had to be strong not just for the family's sake, but to be strong for Ray. I gathered my emotions quickly and followed him out the door.

I stood in the kitchen as Ray's parents stood close by while my father spoke to them. This I could tell was the hardest thing my father ever did. He was not there as the Commander of the VFW, he was there because a fellow veteran, a brother in arms, just lost his son during a time of war. My Dad later told me he felt the loss not just, because the Inslee's were such good friends, but because Ray was also like another son to him. While they talked amongst themselves, I remember seeing Ray's brother, Jimmy walk through the room heading towards the front door. He was wearing one of Ray's Army shirts and the sight of it shook me to my core. Although I held my emotions in check, the look upon Jimmy's face was how I felt inside, completely lost - devoid of emotion. His other brother Bobby was in the living room watching television while Maureen, his little sister was in another room.

Every fiber in my being wanted to cry, but for some reason I could not. I never cried at the loss of anyone I cared about from that day forward. I believe this is when I shut down my emotions completely; because it was the first time, I had ever lost anyone I cared so deeply for. That was one of the darkest days of my life. I witnessed something that day that has stayed with me my entire life. There was something different in my father's eyes, it has haunted me for many years, but now I know what it was. When a parent loses a son or daughter in combat, all veterans feels it deep within their soul as if it were their own child. That sense of loss is what was in my father's eyes that day. This was a sense of loss I would not understand until I took this journey.

Although many of these memories were surrounded by heartache, I never realized how much they influenced my journey in life. Never realizing those memories would lead down a path of discovery, to understand a generation I was too young to know. As I sit here at my computer formulating these words, I know everyone is going to wonder why I would dwell on these feelings or even admit to them. My answer is simple; it is time we as a nation begin to heal. Thanks to the journey I have been on recently, these memories are not so horrific to me anymore. They are part of who I am as a person and they are what helped mold me into who I am as an American. Those thoughts now remind me of how much love, admiration and devotion I have for both my brother Jack and Raymond. Without their ever knowing it, these two men have been my inspiration and driving force all these years. I write this book for them and all the other heroes who have put on the uniform of the United States Military throughout history, today and in the future.

CHAPTER 4
CHOICES MADE BEGIN TO LAY A FOUNDATION

Depending on the opportunities presented to us, we make the choices of our life. We can seize the moment and succeed, or simply allow the opportunity to slither away without ever understanding the real importance in the bigger picture of our life. Maybe it is simply being in the right place at the right time that can help bring us closer to our destiny. Therefore, everything we do in life has a purpose, which helps us better understand who we are, and clarifies our true destiny. Without ever realizing the importance of these moments, one simple choice can ultimately bring a person's life full circle and help unlock the hidden mysteries to our own past.

There were subtle decisions made over the course of a two-year period that presented me with opportunities that make up most writers' dreams. Decisions made independent of each other, but which were actually laying a foundation that would change the course of this writer's destiny. This is when I began to see the true nature of my journey. It created a ripple effect of actions that caused me to take a journey that transformed my life forever. Without realizing the importance of each decision at the time, collectively they placed me on a path to Iraq and on to Vietnam. The totality of these decisions would not be reveled nor understood until I began to transform this journey into words.

The first was a decision to visit the new National World War II Memorial in 2004. Life took on new a meaning while walking through this Memorial in Washington, DC. It was a few days before the dedication and the Memorial was devoid of tourists. The Memorial is spectacular to see in the dark of night, with its subtle lights illuminating each granite panel and the magnificent fountain in the center. The peace and serenity is both haunting and surreal.

While I strolled through the Memorial, soaking in the importance of this period of history, I thought of my father and the men who served with him during the war. How important they were to a small child growing up in New York. Fond memories flooded my mind of tales they shared of fellow soldiers, of stories of what brought them to make the choice of serving in the military during wartime. I recalled stories my mother once told of how everyone throughout the country sacrificed luxuries in order to help support those on the battlefield. These and other memories reminded me of how fortunate I was to grow up surrounded by such wonderful role models. That visit would put me on a quest to relearn that period in history and dedicate a year of my life to the heroes of a lost generation. The lessons learned inspired the writing of my first book *"America United: A Generation's Sacrifice during World War II."*

Since I am a civilian and never made the choice of joining the chosen ranks of our Armed Forces, my research and writings have always come from the experiences of those who have served, along with historical facts. When I began researching the war on terrorism, a few veterans of another war approached me, requesting that I think about writing a book about them – they were Vietnam Veterans.

While thinking about their requests, I wondered how I might include them in the project I was already working on. Thoughts about their requests began to bring back old memories from my childhood. Memories of how the men who served during World War II instilled in me the core values of what it is to be an American.

Closely connected for me was the plight of their sons, the Vietnam veterans and their issues began to weigh heavily on my heart. In 2005, I attended two reunions of Vietnam Veterans – the 101st Airborne and the Third Marine Division. Both of these opportunities not only gave me unique first hand stories to write about, but also gave me new insights into their unique struggles as warriors. During the Third Marine Division Reunion, I met

Bill Ervin, who would later become the critical contact to finalizing the second leg of my journey. The time spent with these men started my mind working to unlock the important key aspect of my research and enhance the journey I would ultimately embark on.

CHAPTER 5
HOW THE JOURNEY BEGAN

August 2005

A week later, my third decision began to pour the concrete for the foundation of this journey. It was during the Marine Corps Reserve Officers Association conference in Baltimore, that I met the man who would extend the all-important invitation. Little did I know, by making a few simple choices, I would have the courage to say "Yes," once I was convinced the invitation was real. Destiny put me on a path to make these choices, but what I was not prepared for was how my life would change and open my eyes to new possibilities.

The conference was held at the Renaissance Harbor Place Hotel, located right across from the Inner Harbor in Baltimore. It was one of those hot, humid summer days and I was glad to be inside where there was air-conditioning. I sat at my table with piles of *"America United: A Generation's Sacrifice during World War II,"* carefully laid out in front of me, waiting to be sold. While I greeted the retired and reserve Marines who filtered by to say hello, I felt completely at ease.

I was deep in conversation with a Major General, when I noticed a young major approach my table. While I reminisced with the General and a few others who had strolled by, the major seemed quite content flipping through pages of one of my books on the table until I was done. I could not help but notice the major smile broadly, when I mentioned I was in the planning stages of a new book, about those serving in the current war in Iraq. When I politely turned my attention to him a few moments later, but before I could apologize for ignoring him, he asked me a question that threw me for loop, "Have you ever thought about being an embedded writer with a unit on the ground in Iraq?" Quite taken aback by his question, and for a brief moment, I did not immediately know what to say in response. As an independent writer, I had not found a way to accomplish anything so grand. Without being associated with a major media group nor being paid by a publishing house there was no venue to get me there from here.

While we discussed my objectives for a future book, we compared the attack of Pearl Harbor to that of the attack on September 11, 2001. We discussed the Japanese objectives of WWII and the terrorists' objectives of today's war. Throughout our conversation, we both agreed, how Americans rallied around our service members back in the 1940s versus the drastic change in mindset of our fellow American's towards service members fighting the current war. Again, he asked me if I would be interested in going to Iraq as an embedded writer with a Marine Corps Unit. This time the answer to his question did not stay on my lips for more than a second.

Major Francis Piccoli, Public Affairs Officer for the Marine Corps'- Marine For Life Program, extended a personal invitation to join a Marine Corps unit in Iraq. His smile said it all as he spoke the words, "Boots on the ground in a combat zone – best experience in the world for a writer!" "Persistent little bugger!" I thought. Just then, I realized he was dead serious. To this day, I still wonder "what the hell" was going through my mind in that moment. Without any hesitation or thinking about the reality of such a trip, my answer was simple, "When do I leave?" He laughed at the quickness of my response and said he would be in touch to go over the details when he returned to his office on Monday morning. Still believing this was a polite invite for the General's sake, who was still standing close by, I blew it off. It was nice to be asked - never in my wildest dreams did I ever think it would become a reality.

Two weeks later, I would realize just how serious he was, when my phone rang and it was Major Piccoli. During the weekend of the conference, Hurricane Katrina and Rita both hit the Gulf Coast of Mississippi and Louisiana, which caused his delay in responding to my acceptance. He apologized and began to give me an update on the devastation down in the New Orleans area. He knew the two-week delay had given me time to consider his offer, and our conversation quickly returned to my going to Iraq.

By this time, you would think I would have talked myself out of it. But, without hesitation, I agreed and asked, "When do I leave?" Once again, he was excited at my response and my eagerness to take such a trip. He began to explain the process. The two weeks had indeed allowed me to think about the possibilities for this type of trip. I knew many of my requests might meet with resistance because of military constraints. Because the conversation with Major Piccoli flowed so easily, I felt comfortable with sharing some of my extreme concepts and ideas.

Mainstream media's objectives, for this type of trip, would be to get their feet on the ground, then twist and turn the stories to fit their nightly news agenda. However, my goals were different. The first goal would be to experience a unit from its pre-deployment and deployment stage all the way through to the Transfer of Authority stage on the ground. The Transfer of Authority is when one unit comes in to relieve another so they can return home to the states. For security reasons, major media is not usually privy to this type of troop movement; this is for the safety of our Armed Forces. A media "leak" of this type of information would compromise our objectives in the war on terrorism. Therefore, I knew my access to these secure movements would be somewhat of a challenge for security reasons. There were many factors to overcome because of my lack of affiliation with a major media outlet. In this, I had one advantage over the media; I had strong ties to the military in Washington, DC. Therefore, if necessary, I could call upon powerful contacts in order to make this trip a reality, and smooth out any snags along the way. There was one problem with calling in those markers – special treatment. I am not one for the special treatment or VIP status when it comes to our military. To me, the troops are the VIPs, not me. The appearance of special treatment could cause much more than ribbing it could create a distance with the troops I was depending on, and make me less effective in objectives. First, I had a lot to say about the war. Secondly, I did not want anyone to ever come back and claim that what I wrote was purely propaganda, or was paid for by the military. This purely would be my thoughts, feelings, observations, experience and journey. I wanted the experience to be the real deal – no dog and pony show.

Other objectives were to experience the process of preparing to go into a combat zone prior to deployment, to live with boots on the ground right along side those in uniform, and if possible, to observe a Civil Affairs Group in action on the ground. This appealed to the Public Affairs Office in many ways - a civilian was willing to tell the real stories as they occurred and not just the blood, guts and gore of war. I got the approval!

It was not until late October 2005 that many of the challenges and roadblocks were resolved. I began working with Captain Miguel Alvarez of the Public Affairs office at Marine Corps Base - Camp Pendleton, and the wheels were set in motion. After receiving paperwork with media guidelines, rules and regulations, and a list of gear I needed to bring with me, my life as I knew it was about to be turned upside down. There was no turning back.

CHAPTER 6
HOW DOES ONE PREPARE FOR A COMBAT ZONE?

I knew there would be changes immediately after I agreed to take this journey. I will admit that I had a mixture of feelings running through me. At first, I thought I was insane for agreeing to take a journey such as this. Then I became nervous as to whether or not I would be able to handle it and survive. There were also the risks involved - I have taken risks in the past but never like this. I found myself in a quandary on what to do and how to prepare.

As a civilian, I had never experienced the process of a military deployment. As an independent writer, I had no one in the media world to turn to for advice for this kind of trip. Panic began to surface and hundreds of questions flooded my mind. Then it occurred to me, I was in a unique position; I had something the media did not have. I had thousands of Marines and Soldiers in my network to turn to for help and advice. Having had the opportunity to compile a strong network of military personnel over the years, I began contacting a few of my favorite Marines and other Soldiers for their advice and guidance.

As word began to circulate throughout my network of active duty, guard and reservists, my phone rang off the hook - advice came to me faster than I could have ever thought possible.

Everyone was excited that I was willing to take such a trip – calling me brave and courageous - I did not see it that way. Each of them were excited, someone was willing to be their voice without being politically biased. They advised to not only think positively, but also remember to consider I could die in Iraq. This last piece of advice was a bit hard to swallow at first, but I knew what they were telling me. One comment was consistent from all of them, "Be sure to have your shit squared away just in case." This advice I took very seriously, because I knew what their warning meant. I had to face reality – I was entering into a combat zone and there was a remote possibility that I might not come home alive.

Although I received wonderful advice concerning gear, how to prepare myself mentally, physically and objectively, there was also the set-up advice. One must understand, our troops have a wonderful sense of humor. When taking advice from someone in uniform, one must weigh all sides of such advice. Take for example one piece of good advice I received from a very special Marine: "Once you get over there, be sure to kick the Head before entering." (In military jargon, the Head is a toilet.) Here was the advice given: "Before entering a port-a-potty, kick it hard, listen for a thud, and if you do not hear one, enter, but be sure to look up and all around before entering." The concept was to ensure that any Camel Spiders that had attached themselves to the interior be dislodged before I entered. This would ensure that I was not vulnerable to their attack once inside. Little did I know, once I was in country, this was a set-up.

On a daily basis, I wondered to myself, "Why am I doing this?" I am in no way a fear- factor chick. I was totally out of shape, and at the age of forty-six, the last place I ever wanted to be was in a combat zone. The answer was always the same – mainstream media is not telling the real stories. In order to write about our warriors, I needed to see the truth first hand.

Mainstream media rarely looks at the bigger picture when it comes to our military – my trip would be to tell the story of our warriors, not just the political side of war. My experience would be different; I would be going deeper than just the story of the Iraq War. This would be a story of those in uniform, living one day at a time in a combat zone. Any fears I might have had disappeared as I thought of the result this type of trip would produce. I did not allow any other thoughts to cloud my judgment and continued to prepare myself for a trip into a combat zone for the first time.

Those in my Veterans community network told me on many occasions that this trip was going to change me forever. My response was always the same, "No it won't." I gained a tremendous amount of understanding and advice from these warriors, not to mention tricks of the trade to survive the trip I was about to embark on.

JANUARY 2006

Throughout many conversations, I realized a few things had not occurred to me before. First, I would probably not know anyone I would be traveling with; I would be very alone. Second, I did not want to be a liability to those in uniform. Media representatives have and always will be a liability to those in uniform because their objective is their story and not the safety of those around them. I was different, because the military was more than a story to me – it was my family and I did not want to be a liability.

As my "to do list" began to grow, a few other things came to mind, and these items began to eat away at me. I knew I needed to make a few decisions in order to put my nerves at ease before I went forward.

I usually travel alone on business trips, but this was no ordinary business trip. I wanted someone with me on this trip for a number of reasons. I was going to need help carrying my gear and equipment. I also needed someone I trusted to tell me the truth and make sure I did not make any mistakes or put those around me in jeopardy for a simple story. I wanted someone I could turn to if I needed to talk, to answer any questions I might have along the way.

Even though I had complete trust and confidence in the Marines I would be assigned to, the thought of going into a combat zone alone began to scare the living hell out of me. I was not concerned for my well-being, but for those Marines around me. I know first hand how protective they can be and I did not want them to be in harms way because I was with them. Call it the protector in me, or maybe it was because of my close relationship with the military, but I would not be able to live with myself if anything were to happen to any of them because they were trying to protect me. Therefore, I made the hard decision to bring someone along with me on this trip. Someone I trusted to ensure not only my safety, but to reassure those around me to not worry about anything but themselves. In making this decision, I had to be willing to put my life in this person's hands, without a question or a doubt in my mind if shit hit the fan. This would be a first for me.

I knew in my heart, I could get through this trip without a hitch, but like my father used to say, "Prior Planning Prevents Piss Poor Performance." He always believed, if you plan for every possible contingency, you would be better prepared to excel in everything you embark on. I have come to realize, his wisdom in that statement has always created productive efforts in my life. Since this type of trip was going to be a new experience for me, I needed help. After several phone calls to the Public Affairs office at Camp Pendleton, I received a "clearance granted" to bring an assistant/bodyguard with me. Now, I had some hard questions to ask myself about the kind of person I wanted to bring along with me.

The process of choosing someone to join me started out as a hard one. There was only one man I wanted with me on this trip, but I had to have a contingency plan just in case he was not available. I needed someone who had four qualities. Someone (1) who was militarily trained for this type of situation; (2) who could listen to his gut, and see things others did not; (3) who I would be willing to trust with my life at the drop of a dime; and (4) who I could turn to, if I needed help with something along the way. In addition, he needed to have a flexible schedule to join me. Once I thought of the qualifications, only three people fit my requirements. One was Army Special Forces, who I knew would never be willing to hang with Marines for a month. The second was engaged in a detail already.

The one person who was on my list was the only person I truly wanted to be with me on this journey. He was the obvious choice and the only one I contacted. He was the one person in this world who I trusted enough to utterly and completely be willing to put my life in his hands at the drop of a dime – Tony O'Brien.

Tony, a retired Navy Lt. Commander, was also a Navy SEAL. He was not only competent and trained for this type of situation, but I knew in my heart if things got hot, he would make sure I'd come home, no matter what. Although it was not easy to talk him into joining me, once he agreed, a tremendous weight was lifted off my shoulders. That one call made all the difference in the world to me – nothing would stop me now from taking this trip. With that out of the way, I began the arduous task of preparing myself to enter a combat zone.

CHAPTER 7
TRUST

FEBRUARY 2006

Many things went through my mind as I began this process - remembering what so many of my military friends said, "Get your shit together!" Trust me when I say they mean it literally, and figuratively. Almost immediately, everything in my life began to change – my outlook on life even began to change. I soon found out, when one begins the process of preparing to enter a combat zone, he or she is transformed into another person altogether. Those in the military find a confidence within their soul they never knew they had.

They rely on the training they received in boot camp and have a special trust in those surrounding them as they begin to move forward into the unknown, all the while knowing they must think of the ultimate sacrifice they could pay – their lives. As a civilian, I did not have the training our warriors have. I did not have that trust factor built into my soul as they have, and I began to wonder, "How do they do it with such grace and determination without ever allowing their fears to show through?"

I began to wonder why this transformation was happening to me when I was only going on such a short trip. One of my Vietnam Veterans answered this question for me, "Because you are about to enter into a combat zone where the variables of life could change in an instant, which makes you stop and think of every aspect of your life." As I looked back on this period of my life, he was right; it was exactly what I was doing. I knew the variables could change in an instant and I did not want to leave anything to chance, or burden anyone with having to deal with settling my affairs.

The word "overwhelmed" does not come close to how I felt during this time. Questions began running through my mind – how do I begin to pre- settle my personal affairs and business affairs? What should I consider as important and what should I put on the back burner? I had no idea where to start first. Panic began to take hold of me.

We all have things in our lives we never want to think about or deal with, but in this case reality kicked in and I had no choice but to deal with them all. As reality kicked in hard, I began to put my mindset into a zone that prevented my emotions from taking hold of me. I realized I had no choice but to deal with everything all at once, and in a very short amount of time. The possibility that I might not come home alive was staring me in the face. This would be the hardest thing I would ever go through in my life. Why was it so hard you might wonder? It is because you must ponder many questions about yourself, your life, personal belongings, and most importantly, your loved ones. Not to mention any professional responsibilities you might have.

One of the lessons I learned in this process was the heavy burden to carry when having to make such hard decisions about one's personal life. The first course of action is choosing the right person to entrust with all your affairs, and if necessary, to carry out final funeral arrangements. As you can tell, I came home in one piece, but at the time I was preparing for this trip, I did not know what the future held for me. Just as those in uniform do on a daily basis, I needed to make decisions that were very hard and not make them lightly.

Throughout this process, I began to relate to those in the National Guard and Reserve forces more than I ever thought I would. What a revelation it was for me. These two groups of service members are the very groups I have dealt with for many years while working with the military.

Trying to avoid having to deal with personal issues, I began making a list of gear and clothing I needed. Unfortunately, it didn't take very long and the issues of personal affairs crept up once again. Even though my checklist included business affairs, my personal affairs seemed to be the hardest for me to resolve. I am not one to trust many people to take care of my affairs except for me, so these were difficult decisions for me to get my head around. To entrust one person with everything you own and everything you value and treasure in your life, is not an easy task. I began to look hard at who I was and at every aspect of my life very carefully.

This is when I began to wonder about a few things regarding our society. Our social climate makes us skeptical about those around us. I began to ponder why trustworthiness was no longer a virtue in our society. Is it because we have become undoubtedly materialistic in our thought process? Are we so fearful of losing our identity that we never want anyone to know the access codes to our financial institutions, or to have access to anything else in our lives that could be easily misused? A most difficult decision for anyone to make, I realized, is to give power of attorney to someone else. Wow, talk about a reality check!

Throughout this process I thought of those in uniform and so many horror stories of entrusting family, spouses or even a friend to take care of such affairs while deployed; only to come home to a different type of reality check – they were not only taken advantage of, but found themselves flat broke or heavily in debt as a result.

No one I would have entrusted with this obligation lived in my state. Surrounding me at the time were many associates and acquaintances who I would not even consider. However, the few within my circle I would were either deployed or otherwise not capable of handling such matters. Oh, do not get me wrong, they could have taken care of the simple things if asked, but I was not looking for someone to handle the simple things. I needed someone who could ultimately handle the hardest thing of all, should anything happen to me.

Difficult Decisions

When one is in a combat zone, it is difficult to handle your own affairs. There is a time difference, no access to phones or the internet when you need them, therefore you have to assign someone you trust to help you.

Handing over power of attorney is a hard nut to swallow for anyone, but it is necessary in order to take care of things when you are unable to handle your own affairs. In my case, I had no choice but to pick one person to deal with not only my personal affairs, but also be willing to take care of some business matters for me while I was out of the country. This person would have to handle everything in my absence, dealing with financial matters, as well as having access to just about everything I owned and held dear. I realized it was a trust issue. I was lucky enough to have a person close to me who I could trust with these matters, and who was willing to handle the most important issue that could arise.

I would later realize that trust would be one of the lessons I needed to learn in this process. Because you must trust the person, you chose to carry the burden of handling your estate and settling your affairs. In making this decision, I picked a person who was strong in both mind and spirit. I did not want this person to fall apart when they needed to be at their strongest. It was very difficult to decide who should take on the burdens of this job. I did not want to offend anyone close to me, yet I wanted to rest in peace knowing the person I chose would have the backbone to stand up for what I wanted. I wanted to be sure that no matter who gave him trouble; my wishes would be honored and carried out to my specifications. He would also have to be willing to take care of my personal effects, distributing them according to my will, and to follow through on the wishes I would leave behind.

Although every warrior deals with this at some point in their career, I began to wonder if my concerns were the same as theirs. Was I really making more out of this process than I needed to? This is when I picked up the phone and called a few friends for advice. It turned out, at some point in a service member's military career; they too had to make these difficult decisions. Many times wishes were not put into writing and were not carried out, because emotions clouded their memory and prevented those left behind from remembering their wishes.

I had two people I could trust with such affairs and one of them was coming with me on this trip. The other was Chuck

Westbrook. Chuck has been a dear friend for many years and worked with me on my first book, America United. Chuck's eye for detail with a camera and a computer is unequaled by anyone I know. Our deep friendship was proof enough; he could be trusted beyond any doubt to handle anything I needed while I was gone. His cool-under-fire approach in making decisions was exactly what I needed for this process. He knew me far better than anyone else did and after many hours of discussing the future of both my personal life and my professional life, he knew what my wishes were far better than anyone was. His willingness to take on this burden was a great relief to me, and it allowed me to carry on with the preparation for this trip. If it were not for Chuck's help, I do not think I would have been ready when it came time to leave. He helped me to remain calm when I was about to pull the hair out of my head. He helped keep me on track of objectives, and gave me suggestions along the way to add to my "To Do List" as the time to leave got closer and closer.

CHAPTER 8
MY "TO DO LIST"

Although I had a huge list of things to acquire for this trip, gear, equipment, special clothing, etc, I had another list of things I felt pressure to resolve before my departure. We all have the proverbial "To Do List," which includes the many things we have yet to accomplish in life. We put most of these things on hold and rarely think about not being around to do them. Maybe it is because we have lives that are much more hectic than they should be. I was no different. My list encompassed things like cleaning out closets, drawers, storage bins, and boxes, going through filing cabinets filled with papers, sorting out legal matters, accounting, taxes, etc.

Before I head out on any trip, I have a practice of making sure everything is taken care of at home and in my office. Again, this was no ordinary business trip. In the past, I have always found that when I am proactive before I travel - I am well prepared, nothing happens and my trip is a success. Well, this journey was not going to be one of those normal trips. This was entering into a combat zone, where the risks of not coming home alive were higher than any typical business trip or vacation.

This is when I began to ask myself many questions; "What if I did not come home? What then?"

We all have those drawers in our lives, the ones we would not want anyone else to go through. Think about it – would you want your friends, family or a stranger to go through your sock or underwear drawer, finding those items you were too lazy to throw out? Would you really want someone to go through your stuff, without your being there? I surely did not. One might call it vanity, ego or pride in one's self to go through one's own personal stuff before leaving on a trip, but I am not one of them.

I made sure there were no skeletons in my closets for anyone to find. Along with "gearing up," I also began clearing out the closets of my life.

As a civilian, I did not need to take this process so seriously, but I did. It was all part of the experience that every reservist and guardsman goes through. Active duty side of the house is a different story. Therefore, I had to face the hard reality of what the future might hold. This was not a walk in the park, or camping expedition; I was entering into a combat zone where unexpected things could happen. The only one who knew if I was to come out alive or not, was the man upstairs. I had to accept the reality of a possible IED, small arms fire, mortar attack, or other type of accident. I had to be serious about what I was getting ready to walk into. While I was given five months to prepare for my trip, those in uniform are usually only given a month's notice. How they can get it all done in that short amount of time is beyond me. One thing I decided early on in this process was to make some changes in my life. First thing I would do, would be to accomplish what was on my "To Do List" fast.

Although it was time consuming, I began going through closets, drawers, boxes and such. As I ticked off each item, I began to feel as though I was accomplishing something, and the process gave me considerable time to think. I thought about those in uniform having to do the same thing. On many occasions, I found myself thinking about the family members left behind, grieving over their loved ones and I began to cry. How hard it must be for them to take care of such matters; what must be going through their minds as they clean out the closets of a loved one who gave the ultimate sacrifice. That kind of loss overtakes their thoughts as their heart yearns for understanding. All the while, they must decide who gets what of those personal belongings. I began to think about this as I cleaned and reorganized. Thoughts of my own family and friends came to mind, and what they might go through should anything happen to me on this trip.

I realized that tens of millions of other Americans had gone through this during all our nations' wars, now it was my turn.

If the person reading this wonders what it is like to go through this phase, take this test– go through your home one day with a pad and pen, making sure to note the time and date you start. As you go through each room, look at every item and make a decision, should that item go to someone or be thrown out? This is very difficult to do when you have plenty of time on your hands, much less do it when you are heading into a combat zone in less than thirty days. When you are done, look over the list and the time you finished. I bet it takes you a few days to accomplish, and you will not be finished. I guarantee, you will add to both lists repeatedly. Take my advice and clean out your closets so no one else has to do it for you after you are gone.

After I purged my life of unwanted items, I realized how cluttered my life had become with materialistic items. We buy certain items for no reason other than to say we own them. All the while, they sit in a closet or collect dust with no real use in our everyday life. When I was done, I looked around and could not believe all the room I had acquired. Wow, what a difference it makes in a person's life. It is extremely freeing to one's soul to clean out the closets of your life. I highly recommend it. Once you get rid of the clutter in your life, your life will begin to change dramatically.

While I went through my cleaning frenzy, I began to separate the items that I wanted to go to certain people and noted who was to receive what. God forbid anything was to happen to me on this trip, I needed to make the process of settling my estate as easy as possible for Chuck. I did not want him caught off guard by anyone claiming I had promised them anything, or that they had the right to something that had belonged to me, just because I was not around to dispute their claim. Therefore, I left everything in writing to help facilitate the process and learned something very valuable from this experience.

The semi-hard part was now complete and I began to prepare myself mentally for what could be. My hat goes off to those in uniform for as they go through this process, their minds must also be on the mission at hand. As I thought about this, I wondered how they dealt with these hard realities of going to war and still be able to have a smile on their face.

After this experience, I believe everyone needs some type of reality check once in his or her life in order to understand what is truly important in life.

[Upon my return home, during a conversation with a soldier's wife, I was told I had subconsciously distanced myself from her and others in the last month before I left. Before being deployed her husband and his fellow, soldiers did this same thing. She brought to my attention, I was distancing myself from those I cared deeply for; it was a very interesting observation to comprehend. I did not realize I had done it. In reflecting on that timeframe, I knew I was busy and maybe subconsciously I created that distance because of what could happen.]

CHAPTER 9
TELLING THE FAMILY

Military people are bound to enter a place that might put them in harms way at some point in their career. When told they are about to go into a combat zone, where the variables and risks are obvious, they are prepared, mentally and physically. It is not easy to hear, but still they are confident in their ability to protect themselves and their brothers and sisters in arms.

As they took the oath to protect and defend, they knew one day they would be called upon to enter into combat, where they might give the ultimate sacrifice. This was their choice to make and they are proud to serve their country. Although they are confident and secure their military training has prepared them for what could be, their family never is.

It is always hard for family members to hear that a loved one is about to enter a combat zone. Their minds begin to wander to the "what if something happens stage." Because their loved one wears the uniform of the United States Armed Forces, they knew the risks were there but still it is hard to comprehend.

The fear of the unknown causes family members to react differently. They will be the one at home reading the paper, or watching the horror on the news each night, thinking the worst. In many cases, someone might say something they will regret forever, while others are more encouraging and excited because you are doing something worth respecting and they are proud. While they try to be supportive and not selfish, subconsciously they think of themselves. It is this fear that takes hold of their heart and compels them to say things they never would have thought to say under normal circumstances. This happens without their ever realizing how they sound and the impact it has on the person who is about to enter into a war zone.

To tell a strong military family such as mine that I was going to Iraq as a civilian without a gun would be insane. They had enough to worry about with other family members who are in the military putting themselves in harms way; they did not need to worry about me too. So I decided in the very beginning of this process not to say a word to my family about my pending trip. I am not in the military, and really had no need to enter Iraq, except that I am a writer and a seeker of the truth – a concept my family could never understand. To enter into a combat zone as a civilian for a story - no one would understand my reasoning or willingness. To me the pen is mightier than the sword and accurate stories are as much a part of winning any war, as are guns and artillery.

Many are not as adventurous as I am and those who could relate were in uniform, though they too might not agree or understand. I therefore kept it quiet until the last possible moment. Why would I withhold this type of information from my family you might ask? Well, to answer you truthfully, I knew emotions would be high and nerves would be rattled; I really did not want to hear any negative reasons as to why I should not take this trip. I wanted and needed only positive thoughts and energy to bolster my strength on this journey. If I had allowed the doubting-Thomas type of comments to take hold of me, I probably would have turned chicken and stayed home. No one could really understand the driving force deep within my soul as to why I wanted to take such a trip; I did not truly understand it myself, but I knew I had to take this journey.

Wisdom

Throughout this process, I continually thought about those who went off to war and never came home. The sacrifices made so others could be free began to take hold of my heart. I thought about a few dear friends who never came home from this war and one who never came home from Vietnam many years ago. I began to wonder if there was a box for writing those farewell letters to loved ones, expressing how they felt deep in their heart on their "To Do List." Many of them never got around to checking that box. I knew from experience that this was the case. Tears began to fall, as I thought of those I have known who never returned alive; never being able to share one last time, what was in their hearts with those they loved the most. I now wonder if they were my driving force in being so determined to write such letters.

The last item on my list was the hardest thing I ever really had to do. Two weeks before I left, I began thinking of the many friends who I cared about and lost as a result of war or unforeseen accidents. The void left behind, from their sudden death, was always a burden to me. It was not just the void of losing their physical being – instead it was the loss of the special friendship; those unspoken words and feelings, which were never shared. We all have our memories of a person, yet we yearn to have something they owned and touched to help keep their memories alive within our hearts after they are gone.

During my last week at home, I dedicated my spare time to writing letters to family and friends. This was a conscious decision not to leave a void of sorrow for those I cared about should I not come home, and I began to write. By the time I was finished, there was a stack of eighty-five letters. This was very cathartic for me as it gave me the opportunity to shed many tears and to void myself of any emotions as I expressed my desires, thoughts and feelings to those who I thought would be grieving if anything were to happen to me.

They all started out the same way "if you are reading this letter, then you now know, I went to Iraq." When one writes this type of letter, you want to bring a smile to a person's face after they have read something like that. You want to leave them with special words of wisdom to help inspire them to move on with life and not dwell on your loss. As I handwrote each letter, I tried to do just that.

When I was done with each letter, I chose an item I had held as a personal treasure and enclosed it for them to hold onto. Once I was done, the envelopes were sealed, addressed, certified, and ready for mailing, if necessary. Even though this was a hard task to accomplish, it truly lightened my heart. There would not be anything left unsaid, nor would there be any void to burden anyone if anything should happen. This surprisingly enough gave me peace of mind to accomplish what I needed to do when I moved forward.

Last Minute Decision

During the same week, news broke that an American female journalist, unarmed and unescorted by military personnel was kidnapped outside of Baghdad. I had received word that the insurgents were gunning for female journalists in order to get more news coverage on American media television. Hearing this news, I began to get concerned as I looked into the mirror. Being a female with long hair, I fell into the category they were gunning for, and I made yet another hard decision – I would shed the locks of long golden hair before I got on the plane. Yes, I sacrificed the hair from just above my waist to just below my ears. Many of my friends freaked out that I had gone to such measures for such a short amount of time. The only thing that was in the back of my mind was the Marines I would be traveling with, and the increased liability I would be to them now. If the insurgents were gunning for female journalists, then I would be a target. The last thing I wanted to do was to bring attention to the unit I would be assigned to. Let's just say the decision was a little added insurance. This decision proved advantageous as it turned out.

Final Thought Before I Left

In the last few days before I left many friends and associates asked if I was getting nervous. I have to admit for some reason I was not. A sense of peace began to take hold of me in those last few days. This was a feeling I had never felt before. As I look back on it now, I think it was because I had taken the advice of so many to get my "shit squared away." Knowing that I had checked off everything, except one item on my "To Do List," gave me the strength to move forward without being nervous. It wouldn't be until I arrived in Iraq that I would begin to understand this strange sense of peace and calm that had taken hold of my heart and soul.

Preparing for a combat deployment is an all-consuming process.

Final Preparation

FEBRUARY 27

It was now the evening before I was to leave for California on a journey that would ultimately change my life forever. Tony O'Brien had arrived on schedule and we went over the upcoming schedule. After dinner, we began checking the gear list. We were ready to rock and roll.

At this point, I was thankful I had received instructions from those who had worn the uniform on protocols, procedures, and what to expect in living the combat life in general. Our men and woman in uniform go through the same thing as they prepare to go into combat, with one exception - they receive military training that prepares them for this transition, where I didn't. I went from the average DC resident to boom, being in a war zone – no basic training for me. Their guidance helped me prepare for this moment. The most important thing I was thankful for was that Tony was going to be with me on this journey.

Looking back on this period in my life, thinking of the headaches I had preparing for this trip; I realized how selfish I had been in the past. As friends were getting ready to deploy, my first thought would be to help them unwind by inviting them over for dinner, or to have a last-minute drink; a few laughs to give them something positive to think about while they were gone. Call it a morale memory. Instead I would hear that they were too busy or some other excuse. I would always get upset because they could not find the time to get together. I felt as if our friendship was not a priority to them as much as it was for me. The process I would go through in preparing for this trip changed my thoughts on this. I was the one needing the emotional morale boost, I was thinking of myself in those situations, not of them. Now I know what thoughts were going through their minds and how they were feeling. Friendships are so very important to each of us, but time just does not allow a person to spend those precious few moments with those we care about before a trip such as this. Emotions must be detached before entering into a combat zone. This is further proof of the kind of emotional detachment necessary to prepare one self to enter into a combat zone.

Surprise Encouragement

Just when you think you know how a person is going to react to a situation, they surprise you and do the complete opposite.

The hardest of people can be reduced to tears when one person, just as hard, says the right thing. I have to admit, I am one of those people. I am completely stone cold and a hard nut to crack with no emotions, especially if I am head strong in doing something. Yet when the right person says something so powerful to a person like me, it is hard not to become emotional.

The night before I left Washington, DC, I received a surprise call from my brother Jack. Jack was the one person in my family I did not want to know about my trip. He had been sick and I did not want him to worry about his little sister entering into a combat zone. As a Vietnam Veteran, Jack saw enough war to last anyone a lifetime. Knowing the hardship he is burdened with on a daily basis, I did not want to worry him unnecessarily, nor did I want him to have a heart attack either when he found out. I am still not sure what went through my mind in how I thought he would react, but when he called me his voice was music to my ears. His words were so encouraging and inspiring, as if something my father would have said, "Kick ass, take names, be safe, do what you are told by the Marines, remember they are your family they will take care of you no matter what." His final words would stay with me the entire trip and gave me the courage and strength to endure the hardships of a combat zone. They gave me such peace of mind and empowered me to be strong – "I am so proud of you for doing this. Always remember I love you and I am with you in spirit." These were powerful positive words coming not only from a veteran, but also from my big brother. He knew exactly what I needed to hear at that moment. Throughout the trip, whenever I would become scared or nervous, his words flooded my mind and helped carry me through, preventing me from ever flinching.

CHAPTER 10
A TEST OF PATIENCE

We all know that since the terrorist attack of September 11[h], 2001, traveling has become a tremendous hassle. Even though the rules are there to safeguard our travels, many people still do not abide by them. One must arrive hours before a flight in order to filter through security checkpoints. All this and pray you make it to your gate on time for your flight. Prior to my arrival at Ronald Reagan Airport that morning, I had taken every precaution to abide by these rules and regulations. I contacted the Transportation Security Administration (TSA) in order to get advice on protocols concerning my gear and equipment. I would not only have camera equipment, but also military- style gear in my suitcase.

I checked in at the counter as directed - three hours prior to departure. This allowed plenty of time to show them my documents and request a hand inspection of equipment by a security supervisor. The process did not take long, and the supervisor agreed everything was in accordance with regulations. He also stated I shouldn't have any problems once my bag was put on the conveyor belt. After assuring me, that the luggage would not be re-opened, he placed a security luggage tag on both pieces; this would indicate to all baggage handlers that they had been hand inspected by a supervisor. I watched as he placed them on the conveyor belt, on their way to wherever luggage goes to in an airport. He and the other personnel nearby wished me luck on my journey and I headed towards the gate.

One has to wonder why security is different from one airport to another. I have traveled all over this country since 2001 and have come to realize each airport's security personnel have different variations to the rules and regulations. Security before you make it to the gate is a whole other story. According to the Transportation Security Administration and the Federal Aviation Administration, all security checkpoint employees receive the same training. As a seasoned traveler, I can definitely say they are not.

Both TSA and the FAA will also say that their security equipment will not damage undeveloped film, believe me it will. Since I was carrying a large amount of film with me (yes I am old school when it comes to photography), I requested another hand-inspection. To help facilitate and speed up this process, I removed all my film from its canisters and placed them in clear zip-lock bags. As instructed, when I got to the security checkpoint, I removed the film from my bag and asked for a hand inspection. The Security person looked at me as if I had three heads, clearly having no clue of what I was asking for and referred me to a supervisor. Since she was wearing a security uniform that said TSA on it, why had she not known what the procedures were? The supervisor at least knew the rules, and the inspection only took a few minutes. At this point, I believed everything was going according to plan; I was in heaven and could now relax.

Arrival into California

Arrival into San Diego Airport was uneventful and we arrived on time. Right on schedule Tony appeared in the baggage area along with our Marine escorts. Things were going according to plan. A short time later, the luggage began to come off the conveyor belt. The large black equipment case came off the belt first and my heart began to race. I patiently stood watching suitcase after suitcase pass me by until the very last piece came off the belt. My excitement diminished quickly when the belt came to a sudden halt. My luggage that contained my clothes and other gear was nowhere to be found. My heart sank. If this was any indication as to how the rest of the trip was going to go, I was in for a bumpy ride.

I will be the first to admit that when I travel, I like things to go without a hitch. This is probably because I am always on a tight schedule and make every effort to keep on schedule, especially when other people are waiting on me. This trip was no different, it was to be extremely tight – arrive at San Diego Airport, gather gear and equipment, drive to Twenty-Nine Palms Marine Corps Base, go through processing, and be ready to leave on the first flight out to Kuwait. Unfortunately, due to the airline's screw-up plans were abruptly changed.

I looked around the luggage area of Southwest Airlines Customer Service while I waited to find out where my suitcase was. There was luggage piled up all around the area, and what surprised me was how many military duffle bags there were – I counted 24 duffle bags in all. Granted, San Diego Airport is located near a few military bases, but still, that many duffle bags makes a person wonder how many military personnel have had to deal with this kind of hiccup over the years.

When I inquired as to where my luggage was and why it never made it on the plane, the blank stare I received was priceless. Although the attendant made phone call after phone call trying to figure out where my suitcase was, still his attitude was like dealing with a person with no intelligence at all. Even though he seemed to go through the motions of trying to help, his "I do not give a shit about the situation" attitude was not only disrespectful, but also devoid of any compassion or sympathy at all. I again looked at the lonely duffle bags sitting outside the door. This again made me wonder about those poor guys and gals who owned the bags sitting outside the door: Were they returning from Iraq or Afghanistan? Were they trying to get back to their duty station? On the other hand, were they just trying to get home to their loved ones while they were on leave?

What got me the most in all of this was the fact that the airlines give out luggage tags when you check in, claiming that it gives them the ability to ensure your luggage gets to the same destination with you on your flight. Yet when your luggage does not show up, this same luggage tag does nothing to help them find your luggage. Why do they give you these tags in the first place? At a time when information technology is so important to all of us to locate everything and anything, why is there no tracking system in place to tell them where your luggage ended up when it does not arrive with you at your destination? This should be considered a security risk, should it not?

After a few heated discussions, the airlines finally agreed to locate my lost luggage and have it delivered to Twenty-Nine Palms.

Although I was upset at the incompetency and attitude of the airline's attendant, I finally calmed down during the drive north towards the base. That is when I realized, the man upstairs had to have something bigger planned for me, and I had to allow the situation to unfold accordingly. A lesson in patience was definitely one of the things I would learn quickly on this trip. I wondered though what I would do about not having any clothes, or even a toothbrush. Our driver must have read my mind, because once we arrived on base, he headed straight for the Post Exchange so I could pick up a few things to tide me over until my luggage showed up. My brother was right - they would take care of me.

Once we arrived at the hotel, the clerk handed me a message to call our Point of Contact, Lt. J.D. Borrero, and liaison for 3LAR at Twenty-Nine Palms. Borrero would be the one to get us squared away with body armor and help with final preparations in order to make this trip a success. After making a quick call to say we had arrived, he advised us there would be a departure of the first phase in the morning, and we agreed to join him to observe the process. We retired for the evening and waited for his call.

My luggage finally arrived in the afternoon of our first day. Although the hand-inspection security tag was still clearly visible, it was evident my bag had been opened somewhere along the line. Upon inspection, many items for this trip were missing. I was not a happy camper. [As I look back on that day, I feel sorry for Tony, having to learn what a hot Irish temper I have.]

I immediately contacted the Southwest Airlines 800-number. They were not willing to accept any responsibility for this hiccup, nor were they willing to listen to my situation. My dissatisfaction in Southwest Airlines' handling of this matter, as if it was not their problem, went beyond my being livid. At my expense, I had no choice but to replace the missing items.

When one goes to an airline's website and purchases a ticket, he or she is purchasing a ticket with that airline. The contract is therefore, between the purchaser and the airline's website. Should anything happen along the itinerary it is the selling airline's fault – in this case, Southwest Airlines. Southwest had a short-lived agreement with ATA airlines for this particular timeframe, and felt it was ATA's fault and not Southwest's responsibility, because ATA was the first airline to accept the luggage. The ole' shifts the blame routine, as my father used to say.

It seems the attitude of airlines these days is to make you feel as though it is a privilege to fly on their planes and not to accept any responsibility but to get you from point A to point B. Tensions are high because of security issues, and as TSA and the FAA make it mandatory that you secure your suitcase only with a TSA-approved lock, which costs anywhere between twelve and eighteen dollars, not finding it on your suitcase upon arrival is a bit unnerving. This makes everything you travel with fair game to anyone who works for the ground crew.

Even after advising Southwest I was about to leave for Iraq and would not be back for a month, the girl on the phone apparently did not hear me. All she would say was that I had thirty days to file a claim with their office, and that she would be happy to send me a form to fill out which I should return to them before they would investigate the complaint. This form was not available electronically by the way. What part of "not going to be in country for the next thirty days" did she not understand? Her only response was, "Ma'am, your travel schedule is not our problem." Southwest Airlines never reimbursed the additional lodging fees, food and replacement costs of the stolen items. Maybe this is one reason's why the airlines are in financial trouble – poor customer service to their air travelers. One has to wonder how they stay in business when they treat their travelers with such disrespect knowing they are far from home.

As with anything in life, things happen for a reason - hiccups always cause stress, but in the end, there is always a reason for them. You would think I would know this by now, but my Irish got the best of me with this hiccup.

CHAPTER 11
THE JOURNEY BEGINS
HURRY UP AND WAIT!

The phone rang early on Friday Morning, alerting us that LT Borrero was on his way to pick us up. A short time later, with camera in hand, we arrived at the staging area - a large parking lot located on base. The lot was dark and cold, with only a few streetlights surrounding the perimeter. For a while, it seemed like we were the only ones in the lot, except for a few Marines. Then the vehicles began to roll in one by one - carrying wives, parents, children, and friends, and the special Marine who was about to leave.

Reality began to hit as I stood in the brisk morning air watching the Marines - all pumped and gung-ho - gathering across the asphalt parking lot. They lined up their duffle bags, three and four deep and high, spread from one end of the lot to the other. This was the start of the waiting game. To a civilian who prides herself on punctuality, I would soon realize that my life was no longer my own. I would have to get used to a lot of hurry-up and wait on this trip.

While I tried to ignore the cold desert air taking control of my body, I began to allow myself to feel the energy, excitement and adrenaline of what was happening around me. I looked into the faces of each Marine as they walked by, hoping to catch a glimpse of an emotion. To some of the Marines it would be their first deployment, while others, more seasoned, it was their second or third. I began to wonder what they were thinking as they prepared to leave their loved ones. Family members were showing tears and every type of emotion; meanwhile, the Marines were not showing their emotions at all. All I saw in their eyes at first glance was a strong sense of confidence and determination.

Occasionally, I saw one who seemed nervous and unsure as he held on tight to those he loved; these were the young new members of the Marine Corps, and it was evident that it was their first deployment. After a while, I could tell who the new recruit was and who had already been there. There is a certain look in the eyes of someone who has seen combat and their facial expressions are hardened; when you look into their eyes or scan their face, you get the sense they have been there more times than they care to admit. They have seen things you would never want to know about.

Even though I was here to observe the Marines and write about them, I decided to switch gears and concentrate my attention on the family members. After all, they were a part of this story too - a part of the story rarely ever written about.

They said their good-byes with tears streaming down their faces, giving everlasting kisses and hugs, and those last minute whispers of encouragement. Watching these Marines say good-bye to the precious little individuals they gave life to, was the hardest part for me. As I watched, I could not imagine what was going through their minds. Having been around the military my entire life, for the first time I saw them differently. I saw them as my brothers, my nephews, my cousins and my friends. Right along with them, I began to get emotional watching as their eyes filled with tears and wondered what the future held for them in that moment. Fighting back my own emotions and tears, I turned my attention to the woman standing next to me, Victoria Sandmeyer.

Victoria is the wife of Lt. Jake Sandmeyer who would be my liaison once we were on the ground in Iraq. She stood in the cold, clutching her son Ezra who was less than a year old in her arms, trying to keep him warm. Her brother lovingly video recorded these last few moments; she was strong and determined to be brave. Yet I could see it in her eyes, she was nervous. I got a strong feeling from this woman that like the others standing around me, they would weather the storm of this deployment with grace and determination to make their Marines proud.

I said good-bye to four other men who would become an important part of my journey in the coming weeks: Lt. Colonel Matt Jones, Commanding Officer for H&S Company; Lt. Pryor who was to be another one of my liaisons; and Sgt Major Lloyd Hatfield, the man who would keep everything moving like a well-greased wheel.

We said our final good-byes and the first group was on their way.

One observation I came away with after watching this deployment was that deployments are not just about going to war; they are much more than that – they're about family! The military is their career and they conduct themselves with the utmost pride in performing their jobs with perfection, but it all comes down to family in the end. They take care of each other before, during and after deployments, which makes the Marine Corps so unique and very special.

Opportunities Present Themselves

Due to our postponed departure, the downtime gave me an opportunity to see the staging of pre-deployment activities for the second phase of deployment. I realized after all, a bigger picture was in store for me. For the first time I was able to get a personal sense of what it felt like to send a family member off to war. Even with all the service members in my own immediate family, I had never experienced this before. While I went through this process, I found myself getting more and more emotional. These Marines were no longer just subjects for a story; they were the men who I would be relying on to protect me. I began wondering if they would protect me or not.

The military hates the media, and I knew they were wondering if I was going to cause them trouble, or be as high maintenance as the last media representative they had on the last deployment. You see in a combat zone, a warrior's mind thinks differently than it does back home. In a combat zone, they wonder if today is going to be their day to take a bullet or who will have the courage to jump on the grenade if necessary. They don't want to worry about someone classified as media.

I tried to separate my emotions from their families during this process, but I kept thinking of those in my own family who are in uniform and could relate quite easily with each of them. I realized I had never been to a good-bye for anyone in my family, and this realization began to bother me.

Among those, saying good-bye to these amazing warriors was a special group of women, known as the Official Huggers. They attend every deployment to give each Marine a hug as they begin to load the buses. This gift of love also gives a special farewell to those whose family is not able to be there. A question rose in my mind, are there Official Huggers at every deployment around the country? I was not able to find an answer to this question. During the second deployment process, these special women would give me a warm invitation to join them in this ceremony. After all these would be the Marines, I would be joining in a few days. This delightful treat gave me an opportunity to bond with them in a unique way.

WITHOUT SKIPPING A BEAT WE MARCHED ON

After spending the day on base going through final paperwork and communicating with liaisons on the other end as to our arrival, we were just about ready to rock and roll. Due to a new threat to female journalists in country, and because some of my gear was stolen, we were issued Desert Camouflaged Uniforms, better known as DCUs in order to secure our safety. This turned out to be advantageous and it would give me the ultimate experience of traveling with the Marines.

The process of being issued body armor and gear was not as easy as one would think. It is like going to a store, with each member of our Armed Forces being responsible for each piece of equipment they are issued. Therefore, you have to check that list carefully before signing on the dotted line and walking away from that counter. Your signature makes you financially responsible for reimbursing the government if anything is lost. I never knew about this process before. I never thought of how it affected our service members in the end, which brought up many questions: What happens in country if someone is injured or displaced from their gear? Who takes responsibility for it then? What happens if it is stolen or damaged? Does the service member get charged?

The Fun Part

Once we acquired our gear, we returned to the hotel so I could get my first lesson in the process of putting it all together. This was the main reason I wanted Tony with me, to teach me the ropes.

Putting the body armor together was a piece of cake - a snap here, a snap there, and I was done. The helmet on the other hand, was a different story.

In order to conserve funding, the United States Military recycles helmets from one war to another. Each one is spray painted green and has a strap mechanism on the inside in order to hold it to one's head securely. Before being deployed, a piece of material is issued that is either green camouflage for jungle situations, or as in our case, digital print for desert situations and must be attached to the helmet. Remember now, I did not go through any basic training where one is taught how to perform this task properly. Being a good little trooper, I asked for assistance. There must be a sign on my forehead that says, "She likes being set up." Because I fell for yet another set up!

Here is how this set up went. There are screws holding the internal straps inside a helmet. They surround the helmet in a circle. Then there is a piece of material that also has slits, which also encircle the perimeter of the cloth. When the piece of digital cloth is placed over the helmet, those slits would lead a layperson to believe the screws should belong in these cuts in order to hold it in place. I spent the next hour and twenty minutes trying to fit this little piece of cloth over the helmet, all the while trying to get the holes to match to the screws.

Frustrated, laughing and cursing up a blue streak, I could not figure out why the screws were not lining up to the holes in the cloth to save my life. Even though I pulled out my trusty Leatherman and began disassembling the entire helmet, I struggled my way through the process. Hey, I was following Tony's lead here. Tony, on the other hand, sat across the room laughing hysterically as he listened and watched me struggle with the piece of material. Tears were streaming down my face, and my sides began to hurt from laughing so hard. Just then, my cell phone rang. It was Lt. Borrero calling to ask if we were ready for dinner.

Although still laughing and crying, I about lost it on the phone, complaining about how it was beyond me that the military could give any service member this kind of equipment and expect them to match up the damn holes. The only thing he would say was, "I will be right there." Ten minutes later, there was a knock on the door and in walked Borrero. Still laughing as he walked in the door, he began looking at what I was struggling with and about fell on the floor at the mess. He looked over at Tony and shook his head. He instructed me to put the screws back where I found them. All the while, he stood there laughing and shaking his head. Once I was done, he took the helmet, placed the material over the top, flipped the helmet over and his next move killed me - there were Velcro strips inside the helmet that held the damn piece of material in place. I looked at JD and then at Tony and could not say a word. Tony just sat there trying not to laugh any harder than he already had, and all he could say in his defense was, "I wanted you to have the full experience for your book." Although I wanted to smack him silly for not telling me how to do it correctly the first time, all I could do was laugh even harder at my own mistake. Hey, he was struggling with it too and I was taking his lead, so I did not think I was the only one having a blonde moment. Hint: never ask a Navy SEAL to put a digital piece of cloth on a helmet - ask a MARINE!

After returning from dinner, I began to prepare myself mentally for the events that would begin in the morning, when it would be our turn to leave. So many thoughts flooded my mind in these closing hours, thoughts of those Vietnam Veterans who told me this experience was going to change me forever, though at this point, I still could not see how. I thought about my family - wondering if there was something, I forgot to say to someone. I thought about the many friends who in the previous weeks asked if I was getting nervous. Words cannot describe the feelings that came over me in that moment. There were no feelings of nervousness or panic, instead it was something very different. As if a soft, comfortable, warm blanket had wrapped itself around me; I was at peace with myself and with God. Then a strong sense of empowerment took hold of my heart. I felt prepared for whatever God had ready for me, including the consequences it would bring.

CHAPTER 12
DEPLOYMENT DAY

It was finally our turn to leave. We arrived at the staging area at 0645. I was now standing in the same parking lot stowing my gear as they had in the previous two groups. Headlights began to come into view through the darkness, filling up the parking lot one car at a time. Marines and their families began to gather in clumps. I looked around at their sleepy faces with sweethearts hanging on tight, storing up those last minute kisses and tender touches to carry them through until their return, when reality hit me like a brick. I remember muttering to myself, "Holy Shit, I am really going to Iraq with the United States Marine Corps." "These are the men I would be entrusting my life to for the next five weeks." I tried my best to separate my emotions at that moment, but I could not. Tears began to well up in my eyes not knowing what the future held for all of us.

Just then a Marine walked by with his hand gently swaying. One finger dangled down and attached to it was a beautiful little girl holding on for dear life as she tried to keep up with her daddy's long legs. Parents and a brother said good-bye to another. A tall redheaded Marine hugged his pregnant wife. My heart began to fill with pride and pain at the same time. Many emotions ran through me that morning, emotions which had built up over the last few days. I began silently saying a prayer for every one of them - for their safety, their serenity, their hopes and dreams of a bright future. The thought of one of these Warriors not coming home to these wonderful people began to cause tears to well up in my eyes even more. I stood around in the brisk desert air for almost three hours watching three units of Marines saying good-bye to loved ones. It was now my turn to hurry up and wait.

With my emotions running high, I seemed to leave myself for a few moments, wondering what the future held for me on this journey. I tried to think of the objectives I wanted to accomplish on this trip. I looked over at Tony and thought about the sacrifices he was making by coming with me. I smiled at how lucky I was to have someone like him in my life – he was a true friend. I began to think about all the single service members who had no one there to say good-bye to before they loaded on the buses. I knew what they were feeling because I felt the loneliness too. There was no one there for me to hang onto either. Although I could not relate to these young men, as I wanted to, I could sense what they were feeling. I turned to confer with Tony, but he was no longer standing next to me. I suddenly felt out of place and a sense of panic began to take hold of me for a brief moment. It was not until I heard Gunnery Sergeant Bivens and Staff Sergeant Cinkosky (Ski), calling my name and was gratefully brought back to the present.

Gunny Bivens, a wiry old salt, was staying behind from this deployment due to injuries he sustained during his last deployment. Staff Sergeant Cinkosky, better known as Sergeant Ski, on the other hand, would be going with us. They eagerly approached with two of their special Warriors and made a round of introductions – Lance Corporal Butterfield and Private First Class Hanson. The Gunny spoke very highly of them in a previous discussion, which was evidence of how proud he was of both of them. "They're squared away and very protective," he said.

Both were in their early twenties with big bright smiles and mischievous sparkles in their eyes. As if it happened this morning, I remember the Gunny telling these guys to watch out for me because I was going to write about them in a book. He told them to be sure I had good clean stories to use. I had to laugh at the half-hearted order being given to them, and I could not help but ask if either of them had any words of wisdom for an embed who knew nothing about going into combat - Butterfield stepped forward and stood in front of me as if he was a father speaking to a young child. Standing over six feet tall, he towered over me - grabbed my collar and said, "Be sure to always wear your body armor when you leave the Forward Operating Base (FOB). Not only to ensure that you are safe from harm -'cause you need to come back in one piece and make us all famous, but because you have a nice rack and we would not want anything to happen to it." I was the only female leaving with this unit, I had to get used to the jokes, and I about fell on the ground laughing at his instructions. I thought the Gunny was going to kill him, but when he saw me laughing so hard, all he could do was laugh at the 'advice' being relayed to me by this very special Marine.

Their smiles and laughter registered in my mind so vividly that morning. It was as if these guys knew what was going through my mind just before they came up to me. Their jokes and laughter were exactly what I needed in that moment. This would be the first of many moments that would register as something special in my mind in the coming weeks.

Although I was laughing harder than I think I have ever laughed before, I took his advice seriously. During the last deployment, Hanson found out first hand how critical body armor was, when he sustained a gunshot to the chest and lived to talk about it. The new body armor plate issued to him saved his life that fateful day.

Time to Load Up and Get on the Road

It was now our time and we began loading the buses. It was my turn to stare out the dirty window, wondering what the future was to hold for all of us as we embarked on this journey together. Outside of Tony, I did not know anyone on this bus and I felt very alone. I listened as a few hung out windows grabbing the last touch of a loved one. I heard faint sobs from a few. No one said a word because many of us wanted to shed a tear, but could not. I thought about pulling out my journal book to jot a few things down, but I could not seem to find the words to put down on paper of how I was feeling. As I look back on it now, it felt almost as if someone else were taking this trip and not me. I remember feeling a vacancy; being devoid of emotions, yet wide-awake. The engines of the buses began revving and we were on our way for the long drive to the airfield and a plane that would take us halfway around the world to Kuwait.

Each time this trip seemed to flow, there seemed to be another snag. When we arrived at the airfield in Riverside, California, the next hiccup arose which almost prevented me from taking this journey. Although we were on the military manifest and listed as part of the unit, the people who took over for Capt Alvarez at the Public Affairs Shop (PAO) at Camp Pendleton had dropped the ball. Knowing I did not have a military ID card, they failed to mention to the group that we were traveling with that I might need some type of ID card other than my passport to board the plane. I had contacted the PAO shop a few days earlier about this issue; their answer, I did not need one. What a mess. This would be the first of many times I would have to call someone higher up and have conversations with the right people in order to correct the errors of this one PAO shop. A short time later, I received the necessary clearance and we were able to enter the secured area. My nerves were now rattled and it took all I had not to return to Camp Pendleton to strangle someone for their incompetency. After awhile I finally calmed down and rested in the hangar with everyone else. This is when my brain finally kicked in and I realized where I was - March Air Force Base, California.

I began to look around the hangar, remembering everything I had read about this base when I was researching for the World War II book. The significance of this base was overwhelming to me. I craved an escape from the confines of this old hangar and felt a sudden need to walk around outside before we left. Talk about an opportunity staring you in the face and not being able to take advantage of it.

March Air Force Base, known as Alessandro Field in 1917 was the original World War I testing site for a new weapon designed and crafted in response to reports from Europe during the war. The Germans had developed a new war fighting capability, air bombers.

A young pilot, while testing one of the new flying machines, Second Lieutenant Peyton March, Jr died after sustaining serious injuries in San Antonio, Texas on February

18, 1918. In his honor, on March 11, 1918, March Air Field received its new name. Second Lt. March, Jr., was the son of General Peyton Conway March, Chief of Staff for the Army and creator of the Air Service during World War I.

March Field was more than just the typical training and testing site over its lifetime – it was the birthplace of the military's air fighting weapons. After the end of World War I, representatives in Congress with a lack of foresight thought differently about air combat and proceeded to institute cutbacks and this base just about became a ghost town. With the creation of the Army Air Corps, in 1926, the base was reborn. Throughout the 1930s, under the command of then Lt. Colonel Harry (Hap) Arnold, the base would again become an important piece of real estate to the military and the civilian world. Because of Hap Arnold, it became the elite base to fly in and out of, bringing notable flying Ace Amelia Earhart, as well as Hollywood's elite, making it a historical icon.

Congress again sought to close the base during another one of its infinite rounds of downsizing, until the attack of Pearl Harbor in 1941. March Field was back in business – this time in full force. Since World War II, this base has consistently stayed an active base. It was a strategic deployment center to Southeast Asia in both the Korean and Vietnam Wars, and was the first place American Prisoners of War landed upon returning home from Vietnam.

While I waited for our flight, I found myself discussing the history of the Base with one of the volunteers from a local veterans' group. It was during our conversation that I was asked if I had ever seen the well-known photo of a POW who dropped to his knees and kissed the ground upon his return home. That very picture was captured right outside the same hangar I was sitting in. I wish I had had an opportunity to walk around the base and absorb the history that once walked through this airfield. I have come to realize one very important lesson on this journey – no matter where you come from, the legacy of those who have served this country proud is in our veins, and that history affects us in everything we do. History can be a very powerful tool if utilized properly.

During this downtime, I also had an opportunity to speak to some of the logistics people handling this troop movement. Thanks to them, I learned about the process regarding troop movement, WOW! If one thinks that our military just picks up a weapon and climbs onto a plane to go to war, they are gravely mistaken. There is a lot involved in transporting thousands of military personnel, along with thousands of pounds of gear and equipment. Logistics of this type of movement would be a nightmare for anyone in the civilian world. Think about it the next time you take a plane trip and what you go through at the airport. Then look out the window as they load your suitcases into the belly of the plane. It is a lot more than just purchasing a ticket. On a military flight into a combat zone, there is tonnage involved; inventory of personnel and food for 350 people for six-mini meals, then add the equipment and gear too. Yet, they do it all with smiles on their faces. Simply amazing!

Before I left the building, I went back to the small group of civilians, veterans, and family members who were there to see that these warriors had a proper send off. Tables lined the walls with donated items such as paperback books, cell phones, coffee, donuts and snacks. After growing up in a military town, spending most of my childhood in the local VFW and American Legion Halls, it was nice to see these cheerful and jovial volunteers representing my two favorite organizations. With broad smiles on their faces, these and many other volunteers come out to assist every flight that leaves or returns from Iraq and Afghanistan. Just when I think I am alone in supporting those in uniform, I get a surprise from small groups such as this. As an American, I can't help but be filled with both pride and gratitude to know that those who have been there take time out of their busy lives to be there for of our service members like this.

Although we boarded a commercial flight filled with military personnel, in typical military style and mentality, there was one exception –the flight crew. The flight crew had flown hundreds of flights over the last few years like this one. I could not help but get a sense from each of the crew that it was an honor to transport these warriors to their destination.

As I settled back in my seat, I thought about the previous few days and what it took to get to this point. One day I wished that someone would explain to me what all this hurry-up and wait is with our military. Until then, I would just sit back and enjoy the ride. It was uneventful until we got to Bangor, Maine.

Throughout this great country, there are small pockets of Americans who actually give a damn about our military and who show it as often as they can. Over the last couple of years, I have heard wonderful stories from many service members about the veterans, civilians and military family members who took the time out of their busy schedules to meet and greet them at various airports as they depart or came home from Iraq, Afghanistan and other parts of the world. I had never met any of these groups before, but on this journey, I would have the opportunity to meet the wonderful citizens of Bangor, Maine. It was strange to live this experience firsthand, because when this journey started to unfold a few months prior, this stop was high on my priority list; although I thought it would be an experience on my way back from Iraq.

The plane landed for refueling and we de-planed. The Marines walked off in two rows. Without their saying a word, they received warm handshakes, smiles and a continuous "Thank you for your service," from the citizens standing on either side of the ramp. The electricity one feels when hearing those words from fellow Americans is the kind of positive energy one needs before entering into a combat zone. Let me tell you, it is a feeling like no other. At the end of the welcome line, a few citizens directed these tired warriors to a special room, where cell phones were available to call loved ones. Everyone on the plane was thankful for the break in flight time.

One special thing about Marines that many do not know is that they are comedians and show-offs. Before we re-boarded the plane, these special Marines showed their appreciation of support to those in the terminal. They stood at attention and began softly singing the Marine Corps Hymn to the citizens of Bangor, Maine. It was the least they could do for these patriots who took time out of their day to come support them enroute to Iraq. There were tears in the veteran's eyes by the time the song was finished. We bid our farewells and gave thanks to the men and women of Bangor Maine, (Betty, John, Mildred, Beth and others), and we were on our way.

[If you ever want to do something to show your appreciation, join a group such as these patriots at your local airport. www.freeportflagladies.com]

CHAPTER 13
BOOTS HIT THE GROUND
KUWAIT

There was no hurry-up and wait once we got to Kuwait Airport. After shuffling off the plane, we immediately boarded buses for the trip that would take us on a convoy ride to the base.

The drive along the Kuwait highway was an interesting one. It was very strange. Even though I was dressed as the Marines were, I had no idea what to expect. The feelings I thought would surely arise, were not there as we traveled across the world. I am not sure why, but I thought I would feel something, maybe a sense of excitement, fear or anticipation, or even a slight rush, but for some reason I felt nothing. The only feeling I had was an all-encompassing sense of calm, peace and serenity. Maybe I was just too tired to notice my feelings at this point.

As the convoy drove down the road, I wondered if it was because I had mentally prepared myself for this trip. Then I looked into the driver's rearview mirror, which was in plain sight, and I looked at the faces of the Marines sleeping behind me and realized why I felt so at peace. It was the self-confidence radiating from these brave warriors, which surrounded me. Although I did not know any of them, I trusted them with my life. I had complete faith and trust in these Marine's, far more than I ever thought I would. To know them one would understand how they trust each other; having faith in their brother sitting beside them. With them surrounding me, and Tony by my side, I felt safe and secure. This was the first time I thought about what Jack had said to me on the phone, – "Betty, trust them, they are your family – they will protect you." A soft smile came to my lips knowing he was right. I was safe.

As the buses continued down the road and the Marines took their short nap, the feeling that captured my heart was of a protective mother for those seated behind me. Many of them could not see outside the bus, the closed curtains protect them from prying eyes. Knowing this, my senses heightened, and I found myself scanning the road in front of us and along side the road. My eyes did not miss a thing. There was a group of men standing along the side of the road watching traffic. At this late hour, I wondered if they were keeping track of troop movements, or if these men were just gathering for another reason. Vehicles scurried around us and I found myself scanning for any type of movement that might cause us harm. I was becoming more and more protective over my sleeping Marines. Knowing there was no need to be worried - we were in Kuwait, a country we helped defend against Saddam Hussein sixteen years before, still I did not trust anyone in this part of the world.

Once we arrived at our destination, trucks were unloaded, gear was gathered and we headed towards the buildings we would call home for the next two days.

I must comment on one thing before I go any further. I had heard horror stories about female journalists traveling with the military. Apparently, they received no respect, had to carry heavy gear and luggage, or told to hurry up by those in uniform. Although my situation was very different from those in the media world, still I found it truly hard to believe that anyone who travels with our military would be treated with such disrespect. I on the other hand, have always had a love for the Marine Corps and our military, and have considered them my family. This trip did not change my thinking; instead, it reinforced it. Each one of the Marines made me feel like I was a part of their unit – a unique opportunity for a writer to have. Each treated me like family and took care of me as if I were their sister. These Marines not only helped me, but didn't even allow me to touch my bags or my gearbox. I did carry my own body armor, (hell, I had to wear it), but by the end of my journey it felt like a protective jacket instead of body armor. I did not want for anything or have to struggle with anything either. Later on in this trip, I would learn the reasons why our media has such a distain for our military and the reasons why they would feel that way.

"Female Marines: The Fewer, The Prouder"

Since the military does not allow male and female counterparts to bunk with one another, a few female Marines took charge of me. These women were on their way to Fallujah and Ramadi as part of an Intelligence team. These five female Marines took control of my gear and me immediately. Welcoming me warmly, they helped take care of me when the male Marines were not around. Over the years, I have gained the friendship of many female Marines whom I have come to admire a great deal, but I had never seen them in action. I would recall those old friends, as these special women in DCUs took me under their wing and told me what it was like to be in the Marine Corps. They are just as gung-ho as their male counterparts, but they remain the woman they were born. Wow, and the way they slung their gear around looked as if they were just picking up a cup of coffee; not a grunt, or a groan from any of them. My hat goes off to the females who answered the call and who are serving in our military.

While the wind howled outside of the makeshift barracks built of metal pipes and wood covered in thick white plastic coverings, we stowed our gear and settled in. With our gear safely stowed, we began gathering outside. Even thought it was just about midnight, blaring floodlights strategically illuminated the area; all I could see was row after row of white plastic buildings lining the area. The area was a long, thin patch of sand edged by wooden planks used as walkways, with floodlights illuminating the desert sky. Even at that late hour, the place was extremely busy with Marines coming and going.

Together we began the long walk to the other side of the base, to a Chow hall for midnight rations. The walk gave us time to stretch our legs and adapt to the atmosphere around us. Even though we consumed a lot of food on the plane, here were 350 Marines gathering in a line to enter a long wooden building filled with tables and chairs, along with a variety of food, salad bar, and drinks. There would be one thing that bothered me about this chow hall, and it would stay with me the entire trip - locals, not our own military personnel, ran it. This would be the first time I felt that unsettling feeling that caused me not to want to eat, but I did anyway. I did not know when we would eat again.

We returned to our barracks and nestled into our cots. Usually at home, I sleep with peace and quiet surrounding me, but this would not be the case in these barracks. This was something I had to get used to, as well as sleeping on a camping-style cot with only a small pillow and poncho liner to keep me warm. While the wind howled outside and the snoring ensued all around me, my dreams of a peaceful sleep would never happen. My sleep pattern would continually be interrupted every three hours by someone new coming into the barracks.

The next few days were transient on the Marine Corps side of this camp. I discovered this is normal during a Transfer of Authority, better known as a TOA. In each barracks, one would expect to awake every three to four hours as new personnel rustled into the barracks. Ours was no different. There would be handfuls of females straggling in at all hours, trying to be as quiet as they could, but after awhile you become oblivious to the noise. For the next two days, I adapted to this schedule right along with them in this quasi holding pattern. Although most would consider this an inconvenience, I spent my time taking advantage of the opportunity of getting to know these female Marines. What else was I to do here, but eat, sleep, watch a movie or grab a few minutes on the Internet to check e-mail? This lifestyle would become a mainstay of my off time in Iraq when I was not typing up notes, interview quotes or journaling my thoughts.

When I was around the male Marines, I recalled observing many of them at the staging area back in California, just a few days ago, in their final moments with their loved ones. The easiest icebreaker to open any conversation with was to inquire who they said their good-byes to. Give any service member the opportunity to talk about their loved ones and you cannot shut them up for anything in the world. As a writer, I could not get enough. They lovingly shared stories about parents, girlfriends and wives, previous trips to Iraq and their goals in life. Hearing their words, I began to see inside their souls, and a stronger sense of pride began to take hold of my heart and my emotions with every conversation. I laughed along with them when they told a joke or two or when they picked on their friends as they told their story. As I listened to their words, I remembered those with tears in their eyes as they said their good-byes in California. Their eyes were no longer soft and tearful; they were now hardened and the tears were replaced with a sense of determination and purpose. Even with the hurry-up and wait pattern we were in, these warriors never faltered on what truly was the mission at hand. Many had done several tours already and were eager to return - their mission was never completed.

At a quick glance, when I looked at these warriors, gathered together in a clump with the standard youth operating equipment in hand, an IPod or game boy temporarily holding their attention, I could see their ages - late teens, early twenties. This view, one would say, represents the youth of today. Yet, if you truly look deeper than the electronic equipment and look past the uniforms, which cover their bodies, you begin to see the Americans for who they really are. They are the best America has to offer. They stand tall and proud and come in different shapes and sizes, of all races, creeds and nationalities. Most are so young, with a few 'older' in their mid thirties and of course, the seasoned old salts, as my Dad would call them, in their forties. They are well trained, both physically and mentally, for what they are about to enter into, a combat zone in Iraq. These are the fighting forces of the United States Marine Corps, and I for one was proud to be with them on this trip.

The trip thus far had been very educational and rewarding to me personally, maybe it is because the special individuals who surround me are helping me to understand another side of this story. I always thought I knew our military pretty well, but these Warriors have opened my eyes to many things. With their help, I have come to realize that I had overlooked many issues in my dealings with the military, things in my heart I knew were either right or wrong, but could not truly comment on because I had not had the opportunity to experience it firsthand. With my eyes now opened, I knew what I needed to do when I got home - Educate my fellow Americans.

Hiccup Time!

With any deployment there are bound to be hiccups, although on a troop level I did not see any major ones that would cause me to believe there were any problems with this movement. It was probably because the leaders were well-trained, very impressive individuals and could handle anything thrown at them. Of course there were little hiccups, little things that would drive any normal person crazy, but not these Marines; they just handled it and moved on. "No time for drama," they said, "Let's just work together and move forward."

One hiccup that had gotten my Irish up during the trip was a discussion at 1600 on Friday by "Lt. Dan" Hitlebitle that we were not going to be able to get on the bird moving forward unless we had new orders. My immediate response was, "How the hell did we get to Kuwait if we were not on orders to begin with?" According to the papers in hand, we were on the Unit's Orders as Embeds when we should have been on Individual Orders as Embeds and issued appropriate ID cards. This was not his fault. The problem was with the same PAO shop, those who originally sent down the directive on how to handle our portion of this deployment. I understood this, but still it made no sense to me to find this out after being in Kuwait for two days. After jumping through a few hoops and contacting those within the PAO shop in both Fallujah and Baghdad, I covered my butt just in case and contacted a friend back in Washington, DC, via phone, and then we waited.

While waiting for a response, I received one email from my coordinating point of contact in the Public Affairs Shop that totally threw me off guard. Talk about incompetency, our Public Affairs Point of Contact, our "Host," had failed to give me one critical piece of the puzzle for this trip - the point of contact who we were to touch base with once we arrived in Kuwait. I could not believe what I was reading. How can you have a guest come to a foreign country and leave them out to hang like this? Lack of communication was apparent and I could see that those in the PAO shop in Fallujah thought they were slick. However, I had a trump card in my pocket that would take care of things and that is who I called. While I waited for further instructions, my thoughts wandered to the media, wondering if they too went through this kind of problem. I would later learn that they have, on many occasions.

A short time later, I received the point of contact's rank and last name with only an organization acronym of CFLCC. They did not provide us with any information on how to get in touch with this person. There was no phone number or explanation as to what the acronym stood for, much less, where it was located. The next best thing I thought to do was to go to the Command and Control office for the IMEF (I Marine Expeditionary Force). I walked into the office and the Sergeant cheerfully offered to help me locate this point of contact. Since I was with the Marine Corps, one would think the Point of Contact would be a Marine, so we started searching on the Marine locator – nothing came up. The Sergeant sent my host an email and asked where we could find our supposed point of contact. We waited a few hours for her reply, and when it came back, we were both shocked. She admitted it was her screw up, she failed to do her job correctly by not contacting CFLCC before my arrival, and therefore they did not even know to have anyone standing by to meet me. 'What a mess!' I thought. After obtaining the proper POC information, we were able to contact the office in order to obtain proper information. I finally learned from the new point of contact what CFLCC stands for "Combined Forces Land Component Command."

After a few conversations with CFLCC in Kuwait and in Baghdad, I realized I was not alone in dealing with this kind of hiccup with this new group of Public Affairs Officers in Fallujah. Apparently, many independent media representatives experienced this in the months since their taking over the area. Independent media to them, are treated as though their considered second-class citizens, unless you are a big name reporter. One has to wonder are trying to secure a civilian job with a big name affiliate when the war is over? Everyone always seems to have a personal agenda. Either way, the media hates the military and the hatred is mutual as well - mainstream media looks for and only wants the blood, guts and gore stories. They are not interested in those who serve. If it is not political in nature, they do not want the story. Many who serve in both Iraq and Afghanistan have given up ever seeing their accomplishments in the media. They know that, the media is politically motivated and will not show the true accomplishments and progress achieved by dedicated individuals who represent all of America. The poor communication and disrespect this PAO shop directed toward me and other independent media who were at their mercy was shocking. As a result, I was compelled to make a call back to Washington, DC and express my disbelief for the situation at hand. The Lt. General to whom I contacted was not happy either and said he would take care of it and for me not to worry. I trusted him much more than I trusted those in the PAO shop Fallujah and went back to the barracks for some shut-eye. I must stress that this hiccup was not a direct result of the military itself, or any reflection on the unit in which we were traveling. It was clearly a lack of respect from one specific Public Affair Shop. This made me wonder a few things.

Looking at the bigger picture, I can surely see now why journalists take it out on the entire military instead of the individuals who were not well suited for their job. Incompetency breeds stupidity and apparently a few of the people I was dealing with at the Public Affairs Shop in Fallujah didn't have the skills necessary to handle their jobs in a combat zone. How they got to the rank of Captain, Major and Lt. Colonel is beyond me. Outside of this hiccup, I cannot complain about anything, because the group we were with treated us with such care and hospitality. I guess this was my first taste of never leaving a man behind, or in my case any woman behind, because they were not willing to move forward without us, and I was very grateful for that.

Later that morning we waited for our turn to load up on the buses to head back to the airfield. Along the drive over there, I prayed that what we needed was waiting for us. A few minutes after we arrived, Staff Sergeant Layman approached, leveling his gaze at me and said, "Not sure what you did, but you both need to come with me." My heart sank for a few moments. We did as he asked and followed him into the Air Officers Building. Once inside, the Air Force Personnel asked for our identification and current travel orders. Although I could not see what he was doing over the tall counter, all I heard was a clicking, as if something was being stamped and stapled. He handed us our identification back, along with a copy of our new travel orders. Once I read over the documents and realized we had received the necessary clearance to move forward, my nerves began to calm down. The call I made back to Washington came through and the orders had just arrived a few minutes before we arrived at the airfield. I had to laugh at the expressions on some of the Marine's faces when they heard I had to call back to Washington for help. I felt better knowing I had a friend in the right place, someone I could call on from a combat area for help if it came down to it. Many thanks General!

We loaded up on the C-130 headed for Iraq, and I sat in the very front of the plane, nestled between two tall Marines. I began watching as they were loading the gear from the back of the plane. I distinctly remember closing my eyes for only a second, and before I knew it; I was being nudged by the Marine next to me to wake up, "What do you mean wake up," I mumbled, "we haven't left Kuwait yet!" All he said was, "Look out the window Ma'am, we're already here." Apparently, after I rested my chin on the neck strap of my body armor, I fell asleep before we even took off from the tarmac. Talk about feeling safe and secure, I never sleep on planes.

CHAPTER 14
WELCOME TO IRAQ

March 2006

It was mid-morning when we landed on the tarmac of Al Asad Air Base, one of three air bases designed for troop transport into the Al Anbar Province area.

"WOW, am I really in Iraq," I thought as I stepped off the plane onto the sweltering tarmac where it felt as though it was a hundred degrees. The first thing that hits you is the air. It feels as if there is none. There is only one way to explain it so that you will understand... the next time you vacuum your home, put your head into the machine and try to breathe. All you feel is dry air and sand. As if like a magnet, the sand sticks to your skin. We directed to a nearby hangar to receive further instructions.

Just before we got on the bus in Kuwait headed towards the C-130, Tony approached and told me one of the Marines just got news he became a Daddy that morning. The new Daddy, a tall striking Marine with red hair was now seated a few spaces from me. We had a few minutes before our instructions would begin, so I leaned forward and looked over at him to inquire about the new member of our family being born. He smiled brightly, beaming from ear to ear and said, "Yes Ma'am, a Boy, Logan is his name, 8 pounds, big head, born at 1800 – all ten fingers and toes too. Wife and baby are doin' just fine Ma'am." I laughed at his response and congratulated him. I remembered him from our wait in California, but I wanted to be certain it was him. I asked if she was the one wearing gray sweats and a white t-shirt when we were leaving, and he nodded yes.

I could not help but smile remembering them at the staging area before we left California. I remember watching this young

Marine and his pregnant wife, wondering why he had not stayed behind another week so he could see his child being born. I had to ask why he had not requested to stay behind for the blessed event, and his response floored me -"Ma'am, my CO offered for me to stay behind, but I declined the offer. I could not allow my brothers to come over here without me. They needed me and I needed to be here for them. My wife knows what my job is and she is totally supportive of it." I did not know what to say. Here I was upset with the military for taking him away from the birth of his first child only to find out it was his decision to leave. Here sat before me a dedicated and selfless American, willing to give up seeing the birth of his first-born child in order to be with his fellow Marines. His unselfishness to serve was an unwavering sacrifice to make! It is a choice many do not understand.

Welcome to Camp Ripper

Once we received our instructions, we made our way to Camp Ripper. This was the Marine Corps' side of the base. The sun was beating down on us as we disembarked from yet another bus. As the flatbed trucks drove in, the Marines began unloading duffle bags and gear. This was another hurry-up-and-wait situation, one of many. There were tall concrete barricades like the kind you see along the highway when the state is doing construction along the road, but these were taller than I had ever seen before. They stood thirty feet tall it seemed, and we took solace in the shade of them, relaxing on our duffle bags, awaiting further instructions. I had heard many describe this place only one way, "What a shit hole this place is!" They were so right. It is a hot, dusty, vast land of nothing but rocks, sand and wind. Nevertheless, this would be home for the next few days.

By now, word had spread that an embedded writer was traveling with the unit, and many of the Marines wandered over to introduce themselves to me. For the next two hours, I would have many conversations that would leave me speechless. Butterfield and Hanson made a point of coming over to check on me, to ensure that I was properly wearing my body armor. I could not help but laugh when Butterfield inspected my gear – I passed inspection with flying-colors. As if knowing my nerves were a bit rattled, Hanson surprised me by softly singing Amazing Grace. What a wonderful way to put our nerves at ease, hearing a velvety voice softly singing the most beautiful song in the world. When he was done, I could not help but give this young Marine a hug. His smile warmed my heart more than the heat in the air.

Others gathered around and we chatted about everything and anything that came to mind as we waited. The more I got to know these warriors, the prouder I became. They had the best sense of humor and attitudes about what they were about to get into. They were pumped and ready to rock and roll if necessary. Their mission is foremost in their mind, especially to those who are on their second or third tour. They are ready to finish the job they set out to do a year ago when they left here; help to finish freeing the civilians by securing and rebuilding Iraq. Their stories of being a part of the rebuilding of a country were not only motivating but also inspiring.

Through the hardened lines of their faces, warm smiles shined through as they told stories of rebuilding a city – creating or building from scratch, new medical facilities, schools and water treatment plants.

One Marine, LCpl McLaughlin, whom I nicknamed Hollywood because he had the face, eyes, and smile of a movie star, was also a comedian, lounged in the sun listening to his IPod. Another Marine expressed his excitement to be returning to the Haditha area. He had been there when they first entered the country and took control of the Haditha Dam.

The Dam, which used to provide electricity and water for the region before Saddam took control, had not worked since the early seventies. Saddam's reign disabled it in order to help him control those he was oppressing.

"The civilians in this area haven't had running water or electricity for over 37 years," he told me.

It was just about finished before he left, but he never had the opportunity to see it in working order. He was so excited to finally be back and get to see it in all its glory and splendor. The sparkle in this Marine's eye, as he talked about his time at the Dam, was like watching a child playing with a new toy. Another Marine said he could not wait to return to Rawah to see if the medical facility he once helped guard, as the Navy Seabee's were rebuilding it from the ground up was getting along. "Was it helping the children in the area?" he wondered aloud. This brought up another set of questions for those who were returning; "What about the children of this country?" They talked about the children of this country as if they were their own offspring. One said they reminded him of his own kids back home. "They're so young, impressionable, and so filled with hope for a better tomorrow."

Training the new Iraqi Army and ensuring they have the training to succeed brings a smile to the faces of these brave Warriors. When asked why he was so excited to come back here, Hollywood responded, "Ma'am, I am an American history nut. Just think if you could have been in America during the 1700s, being a part of the birth of a new nation, creating a new country from oppression and tyranny. This, Iraq's Freedom, is kind of, like what America went through during the 1700s. I am excited to be a part of this new country being created. To help those who live here have water for the first time, to have electricity for the first time, and most importantly, to vote for the first time. This is an exciting time for them and I am proud to be a part of it." I sat among these warriors listening to their words, not knowing what to say in return, and then I looked around at the others, who were nodding in agreement. Here before me was a man all of 20 years old comparing our country's independence to that of the Iraqi People. Wow, I was shocked that someone of his age would even think of such a thing. I was speechless for a moment as my heart filled with pride and admiration for his way of looking at the situation at hand. Seeing the smile on their faces as they nodded in agreement made me want to cry at their passion and dedication to the effort and change in this country. I wondered why the mainstream media would not capture this type of story and show it to the world.

This would be the last time I would see many of these Marines, as they would be scattered around the area to different Forward Operating Bases, better known as FOBs.

When one thinks of a forward operating base, the image of the old television show MASH comes to mind, with its flimsy tents, wooden latrines and tent style chow halls. Camp Ripper is nothing like what you would expect from a Hollywood-style FOB. Located west of Baghdad atop an old quarry bed sits Camp Ripper. Picture a gravel driveway with small gravel pieces and think of how hard it is walking on them. Then enlarge the gravel to fist size pieces and you have the ground at Camp Ripper. If one is not paying attention to where he is walking, he could end up with a broken ankle. All the while, it is hot and dusty with no humidity in the air at all.

Although this is a permanent base, it is also a transition base where personnel stay for one day before heading out to their permanent duty station for the duration of their stint in Iraq. It is not the best place to be, but to these warriors its home.

The weather in this part of the country during the month of March is decent to those who live here. This is before the serious hot weather sets in that can astound you if you are not ready for it. Prior to our arrival it was the rainy season and from what I heard, I was glad we arrived when we did. We would be lucky with the weather, because of the timeframe we were there. It was cool in the evenings and about 80 degrees during the daytime, with very little wind. Due to the lack of moisture in the air, dehydration happens very quickly, since you do not feel yourself sweating; your skin is always dry. Therefore, drinking plenty of water is essential to staying alive in this place.

Operations inside the base were nothing like the television newscasts I had seen back home. The area happened to be secure, with the exception of a few sporadic mortar attacks, which reminded me that I was in a combat zone.

Once we found our sleeping quarters - the Marines to their barracks, I to the VIP quarters. Not what I expected in a combat zone I must say –I lived in a "CHU," a container-housing unit, or Can. Picture two small storage units set side by side, each with a door and a window. Toilets/showers are just outside the door. This will be my home for the next few days. These Marines know how to treat a lady! Tony stayed in the Barracks. I was actually jealous; he was able to spend so much time with them, when I was the one here to write about them.

First Chow Hall Experience in a Combat Zone

This and all chow halls in the country are run by KBR (formerly Kellogg, Brown and Root), which is a subsidiary of Halliburton.

While I waited in line to enter the building, I began thinking about KBR's long history of working with the military, which dates back to its original owners, Brown and Root. The Texas based Engineering and Construction Company won many contracts with the Navy in the early nineteen hundreds.

Brown and Root was acquired by Halliburton in the early sixties, and shortly after President Kennedy's assassination, Halliburton's newly acquired company won even more contracts, one specifically to help rebuild the infrastructure in Vietnam for the United States Army. It has always been rumored the contract, as well as others were awarded as a payback from President Johnson for their supporting him throughout his political career.

Brown & Roots affiliation with political influence dates back to the depression years when they first met a new up and coming candidate for Congress, Lyndon B. Johnson. Their affiliation with Johnson gained them higher access to then President Franklin D. Roosevelt, which resulted in the utilization of federal funding resources and changed many laws dealing with the Bureau of Reclamation. These changes allowed for the manipulation of federal funding use on private land for the Texas Colorado Dam. This helped advance Roosevelt's efforts with his New Deal Act back in the forties.

Brown and Roots' initial affiliation with Johnson was not only profitable; it gained them the political influence they craved. As a result, they won contract after contract from the War Department to build many military installations during World War II, as well as shipbuilding and then offshore oilrig platforms. The power they wield also helped deflect an Internal

Revenue Service Investigation; the allegations claimed writing off campaign finance contributions to Johnsons' Senatorial campaign as business deductions. This could have been disastrous to any future political campaign for Johnson. Rumors around Washington were that after a private meeting between Johnson and Roosevelt, the Internal Revenue Service was quietly asked to shut down their investigation directly by President Franklin D. Roosevelt.

I am not sure what I expected when I first entered the chow hall, but as I walked into the building, the hair on the back of my neck stood up. Usually when this happens, it means people in the room are not to be trusted. I was not sure at first why I felt this way, but after entering the building, I began to see the reasons why.

Picture an extra large, construction-style trailer that spans a quarter of a football field with tables and chairs lined up cafeteria style. Throw in a buffet-style food line, drinks in upright coolers and a salad bar. Fruit, snacks and such scattered around, along with the legendary ice cream cooler I had heard so much about. Pink and white light fixtures lined the ceiling - God only knows why.

The food in the Chow Hall was ok, if you like everything boiled. Although, I did not have a problem with the food or the layout, however, I did have a problem with the workers who were scurrying around. The workers were not Americans; they were employees of KBR. They were either locals or from other countries in the region. I felt as though they were continually watching me, which made their presence very uncomfortable.

I looked around the room at the Marines eating their meals and got an uneasy feeling from them as well. They seemed to have a look about them as if to say, let me eat my meal and get the hell out of here as soon as possible. One night after dinner, I was sitting outside my can with a cup of weak coffee and a cigarette, gathering my thoughts when a group of Marines walked by. They stopped to ask for a light for their cigarette. One of them asked if I was the writer who was visiting them. I laughed and of course said "Yes." We chatted for a while talking war stories and what they were feeling about being there. Knowing this was my golden chance, I asked them what they thought of the Chow Hall across the way. Puzzled, they wondered why I would ask such a thing. I began to relay my feelings, of how it made the hair on the back of my neck stand up every time I walked into the building. I asked if I was feeling this way unnecessarily, when one Marine interrupted me and said, he felt that way. Another said when he goes in, he eats and gets out fast. He could not seem to relax in there. Another said he cannot cut up with his friends and surely cannot talk about work in there. I asked them all if they felt the same way, and they admitted they did. "There are too many locals on this base and that makes us all uncomfortable. We do not trust any of them, no matter what country they come from." One Marine said adamantly. I had to agree with him on that observation.

Another contractor on base who was required to clean out the toilets/showers employed locals as well. One morning while I stretched outside my can, I watched one small group of these workers as they cleaned out the toilets in front of my can. I watched as they removed the garbage can from the building and began rummaging through its contents. One individual removed a piece of paper and put it into his pocket. Only after the flash from my camera went off, did they realize I was watching them. I immediately went back inside and downloaded the picture to my laptop, copied it to a disk and walked it over to the Commanding Officer of the base. After I alerted him to the situation and gave him the evidence, he was not happy about my observation, but was very grateful for letting him know there was a possible breach of security. I never saw those workers again after that day. (I would later learn those workers were fired and replaced with a new group of workers.)

Meanwhile, we were in a holding pattern awaiting clearance to fly to Baghdad for the infamous media credentials. Our new hosts of RCT-7 were great, ensuring we were comfortable, well fed and enjoying our stay on their base. Our new Public Affairs host's were wonderful. They surely knew their jobs and were eager to help ensure that we are able to maximize our efforts while on their base. If it were not for the quick thinking of Capt Alvarez and Staff Sergeant Jim Griffin, this holding pattern would have been a waste. They lined up meetings with various groups scattered around the base for interviews. Without them, I would not have been able to capture the essence of another set of the Warriors' life in this area.

CHAPTER 15
ACCOMPLISHMENTS

The first thing that comes to anyone's mind when they hear the term "War in Iraq" is to think of the stories we read in the paper, or see on television: IEDs, bombs, deaths and other horrible things. Unfortunately, what we never hear about are the amazing accomplishments achieved on a daily basis.

During my time at Camp Ripper, I had the opportunity of talking with three groups of warriors; a Naval Reserve Engineering Battalion, (Seabees) the Marine Corps' 3rd and 6th Civil Affairs Groups, and the Combat Photographers of the United States Marine Corps. The last are a very special group of Marines who help capture the history and life of those in a combat zone. These men and women are the most dedicated individuals I have ever met; they capture historical events that help show the transformation of a country – talk about dedicated Warriors.

SEABEES:

Whenever I hear the term "Navy Seabees," my mind wanders to an old John Wayne movie called "The Fighting Seabees." This was a movie about a team of men during World War II, who were recruited by the Navy, to form a new construction battalion. During the movie, John Wayne's mission was to put together a team of skilled artisans, known not for their fighting strength, but for their skills. They needed to be able to erect not only buildings, but also everything from bridges to airfields. Even as a young child, I could grasp the essence of this movie and appreciate how they built the airfields and living quarters on the islands in the Pacific. I always wondered though, if they really existed or if this was just fantasy.

Following in the tradition of "The Fighting Seabees," these dedicated, highly skilled artisans really do exist. They are reservists of the United States Navy, skilled tradesmen in their industries – plumbers, electricians, welders, drivers, construction workers, engineers, and so much more. These talented reservists have now brought their talents to Iraq in the tradition of their units – enduring enormous amounts of enemy fire while following Marines and Army personnel into battle areas. Even while the fighting is still going on, they begin building major airstrips, bridges, roads, gasoline storage tanks, and Quonset huts. Quonset huts serve a variety of uses, as offices, warehouses, hospitals, and housing, thereby creating a new Forward Operating Base that the warriors call home. This war is no different from any other battles they have encountered. As our troops came into Iraq, so do the infamous Fighting Seabees! Today they are using their talents and traditions as they build sleeping quarters and erect buildings and even airstrips for their fellow warriors to fight quickly, stronger, and more efficiently in and around Iraq.

During a media briefing with this unit, I learned of their activities in Iraq. I learned how they transformed what used to be just sand into many of the forward operating bases throughout the country. These Seabees, and those before them, have left their fingerprints all over the Al Anbar Province – from as far north as the Euphrates River, where they reconstructed bridges, roads and outposts, to one specific dam, which this unit and the units before them are the most proud – the Haditha Dam. During the briefing, I could see the transformation of the Commanding Officer's face as he began to describe his first tour at the Haditha Dam. It went from a far-off, distant gaze to one of pure excitement in a matter of seconds. Accompanied by a Marine unit together they secured the dam, which allowed his unit to begin the process of rebuilding. With bullets flying overhead, they began to clean out and rebuild the infrastructure of the dam itself. "It was a rough time at first," he said, "they fought us tooth and nail." "What about now?" I asked. "They love us in that area now," he replied. A sense of personal pride and accomplishment came over his face when he said, "They have water and electricity for the first time in thirty-seven years." After seeing the pictures showing the transformation of the area, I began to understand what the Marines were trying to tell me earlier. I now understood why they were so excited to see it in all its glory, finally working again. Although I wished they were with me to see those pictures, I knew they would be seeing it shortly as they began to patrol the area once again.

There is not a forward operating base in the country that the Seabees did not create. Not only have they built forward operating bases for our military, they have fixed or rebuilt electrical systems for both our military and the Iraqi people. Together with their counterparts on each base, they have built hospitals, bridges and schools in record time to ensure the quality of life for local residents. As you go around the country to any of these bases, you can see the work of these brave men and women, for their signature is all over the place. It was nice to see that they are continuing the legacy of John Wayne and "The Fighting Seabees! A job well done!

As I drove away from the building, I thought about my life back in the States. I could not imagine that life without running water for one day, much less thirty-seven years.

CAG: Civil Affairs Group

While the Seabees rebuild structures, the Civil Affairs Units (CAG) rebuilds lives. This group is a specialized team of the Marine Corps', which goes deep into the community to learn about their way of life. Let me just say, this group can be likened to a community outreach team, and there is much more to them.

Each member of this unique group has worked in the private sector in some capacity of business: infrastructure, communications, legal system, or law enforcement. They each bring a different set of skills to the table in order to benefit a community in rebuilding after the fighting is over. Many times the relationship that is built between these CAG warriors and community members reaps rewards far beyond anyone's comprehension. Those within the community begin to understand that the Americans in uniform are there to help them, not harm them. These realizations begin to help to combat those insurgents who wish to cause additional harm in the area.

According to the United States Military Doctrine, which defines Civil Military Operations (CMO), "the activities of a commander ... establish, maintain, influence, and/or expound relations between military forces, governmental and non-governmental civilian organizations and authorities and the civilian populace in a friendly, neutral or hostile operational area in order to facilitate military operations." In the US Marine Corps, Civil Affairs Units are comprised of "active and reserve component forces and units organized, trained, and equipped specifically to conduct Civil Affair activities and to support Civil Military Operations."

In nonprofessionals' terms, this means that Civil Affairs Marines help the Commander deal with all aspects of local populations and civilian authorities during military missions. Civil Affairs Marines follow frontline combat units into battle to help with the after effects of combat. They also put a kinder face on the ugliness of combat.

From a U.S. Marine perspective, combat is a two-handed approach. One hand is a balled fist to destroy the enemy, while the other is an open helping hand for the displaced, the weary, and the unfortunate. All Marines play their parts in being "ambassadors in uniform," but Civil Affairs Marines go deeper into the community.

Marines in a Civil Affairs Unit are not only hard chargers with the mission at hand, but also are kind with hearts of gold. Often times it is easier to be a Marine in a rifle squad concerned strictly with mission accomplishment and the fighting at hand, rather than to deal directly with the tragedy of war. While regular line units are mainly concerned with the actual war, the fighting part of combat, their work usually stops when the last round is fired. For a Civil Affairs Marine, his job begins when the fighting ends. He mitigates the damages of high-power weapons, and the inhumanity caused by collateral damage from both enemy and friendly forces.

A Civil Affairs Marine is a jack-of-all-trades, from helping pregnant women deliver their babies on a battlefield, to delivering the bodies of civilians killed in combat back to loved ones who survived, to helping local officials arrange truces between rival factions to rebuild a new local government. Civil Affairs Marines can expect such varied situations that not every eventuality can be prepared for, and therefore they must be able to quickly assess the situations and think on their feet.

Civil Affairs Marines are trained to conduct the following missions:

- Population Resource Control
- Foreign Nation Support
- Humanitarian Assistance
- Humanitarian and Civic Action
- Military Civic Action
- Civil Defense
- Civil Administrations

In Iraq, these missions can be:

- Going in with the combat force to route civilians safely out of the fighting, while keeping the roads clear so military forces can quickly move forward.
- Working with local shopkeepers to provide infant formula for babies born in humanitarian camps that were set up to help civilians displaced by the fighting.
- Restoring essential basic services within a town (*i.e.*, water, electricity, medical and shelter) to make the town habitable after the fighting has ended.
- Starting town-cleanup projects, getting local governments up and running again.

When local government is lacking or ineffective, it is the Civil Affairs Marines' job to get it working. When a Marine infantry unit moves on to a new fight, it is the Civil Affairs Marines who stay with the locals to make sure things work.

COMBAT PHOTOGRAPHERS:

I described combat photographers in my World War II book

as special, because they are the dedicated individuals who capture the essence of our military during wartime. They capture the raw feelings of those in uniform, while capturing the hearts and souls of those who are fighting for their independence and survival in a war-torn country. They are the military's historians behind a lens who give us the opportunity to see war through their eyes. Many of their pictures and stories are horrific, but more times than not, they are of the people who are fighting for their lives – both the civilians and our military.

Their job description is to go out on patrol and look for the heart and soul of a community. They are dressed as military personnel and carry a weapon, but they also carry the most important weapon of all – a camera. Their eyes are the lenses, which capture history in a brief moment, and bring back the stories I wish our media would utilize. It is their photos and footage the media uses on the nightly news; yet the real stories are never given. They are the ones who venture onto the battlefields and return with vibrant stories of accomplishments, loss and bravery that should be told each day. Yet others use them differently.

I had the honor of spending time with these brave warriors while at Camp Ripper. One in particular touched my heart – LCpl Benjamin Flores.

Flores is a tall good-looking Marine in his mid-twenties. Even though I tried to get him to talk about himself and his time in country, he would not have it. He was not interested in talking about himself or life in Iraq, but rather his mentor – Cpl. William Salazar. To him, Salazar was everything a great combat photographer should be. Salazar was his motivator, teacher, and challenger when he first entered the Combat Photographer School in Maryland.

As he looked off into the distance, Flores said, "He knew his craft better than anyone else at the school. He was always interested in making his fellow Marines look good. He was the most squared away Marine I have ever known. He was a hard ass, but he took me under his wing and trained me the right way – encouraged me to be creative and to capture the soul of the situation when taking a picture." He paused for a moment, then went on to say, "He was college educated you know. He could have been an officer, but he wanted to be a grunt and make a difference in the world. Friends looked up to him and he challenged them too." As he spoke the words, the far off look changed suddenly, and he began to describe the day he heard the news. He was at the Blue Diamond FOB when the Warrant Officer came into the office. "That look upon his face," he said, "will never be forgotten. I will never forget that day; it was 15 October 2004. He spoke the words that Salazar had died from wounds sustained in battle, and I immediately thought I was dreaming." His eyes closed suddenly as the emotions began to rise in his throat. "He was the first combat photographer to get hit over here. He was one of us and we all felt the pain and loss." The far-off gaze took hold of Flores once again as he continued. "He was rough, but soft in the heart you know. He would loan you money if you needed help. He wanted to extend his tour so he could ride 'til the wheels fell off this train. He wanted to show the world the accomplishments we were achieving over here." Then he began to laugh suddenly. "He was a member of a mariachi band back in California and loved to make us laugh. He could not hold a grudge to save his life and was so proud to be a Marine. Every time I go out to cover an area, he is with me, challenging me to find the picture that will tell the story. Everything I am as a combat photographer is because of him."

His words stayed with me the rest of the trip.

Meanwhile, in other parts of the country, soldiers of the U.S. Army and Army National Guard are helping to make improvements to help villagers. In the southern region of the country, farming cooperatives have begun, to assist Iraqi citizens in cultivating their land in order to produce food to feed their families. Waterways that used to provide water for crops and animals in the area have been cleaned or reconstructed, and are again working at full capacity. Electrical transformers purchased from German manufacturers and installed in and around Baghdad would short out nightly, because they had not been maintained properly; are now being maintained to work at full capacity.

The accomplishments made on a daily basis seem to go unheralded by the mainstream media, while the same blood and guts stories lead daily on every American news channel. WHY?

Sleeping Through an Attack

You would think that I would not be able to sleep soundly in a combat zone; but in fact, I was able to sleep like a rock, with the exception of someone coming into the quarters next to me. On one particular night, I awoke to a knock at the door. I looked at my watch and it was nearing midnight. Stumbling in the blackness of night, fumbling around for the key, I finally opened the door only to find Captain Alvarez standing on the other side. He calmly advised me that we were under a small-arms fire attack. Since I was still semi-asleep, it did not register with my brain. He asked me not to leave my can; but I knew it was an order. I agreed and stumbled back to the rack. I lay back down, still groggy, briefly wondering if I should put on my body armor that was on the other side of the room. At this point, it would have taken a lot for me to get back up and stumble in the dark to where the armor was sitting. I ignored it and rolled over and went back to sleep. The next morning I awoke to find out that three, 122 millimeter round mortars had hit the other side of the base. There were no casualties or injuries, thank God, as the insurgents apparently did not know how to launch properly. This was the first attack since October on this base; yet to those on the base, it was just an annoyance of broken sleep. As for me, I slept right through it. Either I was so exhausted it did not faze me, or I felt safe and secure where I was. I am still not sure which it was, but I did sleep right through it. Later I felt guilty because I didn't even think of Tony being on the other side of the base and I had his body armor in my room.

Traveling Around the Area

In a combat zone, traveling from one location to another is not easy. You can't plan for a short trip by hopping on a plane and arriving in a few hours. Logistics in getting from one place to another is a lot harder than one might imagine. It can take one day, or five days, to get approval to board a flight. Priority personnel get first dibs on flights out of an FOB; media guests are not priority passengers, for obvious reasons.

While we played the hurry-up-and-wait game, and tried to get to Baghdad to acquire our media credentials as directed, to accommodate those in Fallujah, it was not in the cards to do so. Each night we would pack up our gear and haul it over to the airfield, only to sit in the hangar until the bird landed. If I ever hear the words, "You're good to go" again, I will probably scream. Now remember, I am the one who is a stickler for schedules. It was very humbling to realize that the situation was beyond my control. After awhile, "You're good to go" began to take on a completely new meaning for Capt. Alvarez and I. Once he uttered the words, I knew we were not going anywhere. By the third night, I would joke that he had better not go to sleep early, so he could come back and pick us up by 11 p.m. We both would laugh at the reference, but he figured he would get a call after awhile, and he did.

Although I was the one on a short schedule and needed to obtain what I needed before we left the country, I soon realized a very important lesson – it was not about me, it was about the mission. Therefore, I learned to have patience in dealing with the hiccups of traveling in a combat zone. It is all a matter of priority and we were not on the list.

At this point, I realized it was going to be impossible to get to Baghdad. It was about a ten-hour drive from where we were, across vast desert terrain to where we needed to meet up with the Marines once again, and there were no cabs available to take us there. However, we regrouped and found alternative transportation that was heading to the area where we needed to link up with the Marines once again – a convoy of the Maryland Army National Guard transporting supplies to the western part of the country. We jumped at the chance. A convoy – I must be nuts!

For a brief few moments, I recalled the many stories of unsuccessful convoys attacked by insurgents along the roadside, and the infamous IEDs that were all over the news on a daily basis at home. Part of me wanted to scream out 'NO

CONVOY!', but so much time had already been lost waiting for transport to Baghdad. The threats dimmed as I focused on wanting to continue my journey, to get the stories I was here to tell. Finally, after much deliberation with myself, I agreed to join the convoy.

On the morning of our departure, we met the group of Army National Guardsman whom we were joining on their journey across the open desert. I could not believe that I was in Iraq, and neighbors from back home would be taking me to the heart of Al Anbar Province. Talk about luck. These Soldiers were great; they welcomed us warmly and promised to take every precaution to get us to our location safely. They had reason for being cautious – they were due to go home in a few weeks.

Before we set out on the road, without sounding corny, I asked the Captain and Lieutenant if I could meet those who would be riding in the lead and rear vehicles, as well as the corpsman for a brief moment so that I could give them something special. Both complied without question. Once they arrived, I asked each of them if they were religious or spiritual in any way. Each said they were. I reached into my bag and retrieved a small bag filled with white cloths. They were handkerchiefs that a friend's father, a minister, had sent to me prior to my taking this journey. The minister's congregation prayed over the handkerchiefs for the safety of all those who traveled around with us. I received special instructions to hand them out when I deemed it appropriate. The convoy definitely felt like appropriate timing.

We were about to take a very special trip, and I wanted each one to know, some very special people back home were praying for their safety. I proceeded to hand out the prayer cloths to each of them, and since the corpsman knew this was my first convoy, and I would probably be a bit nervous; he offered to say a short prayer for our safety. We joined hands and bowed our heads while he spoke.

As I lifted my head, I looked at the sky, as if it was a message from the heavens, the Doc and I just looked at each other in amazement – the beauty of the sunrise surprised us all.

It was the most breathtaking ray of sunlight peaking out from behind the clouds I had ever seen in my life. I grabbed my camera and took a picture of the view before my eyes. We left each other and began loading the vehicles. During the trip across the desert, the feeling stayed with me. Whenever I look at that picture, I can still feel the warmth I felt in the moment, a feeling that to this day is still with me.

The convoy was comprised of 132 vehicles filled with supplies, food, water, and fuel trucks, mostly commercial vehicles bringing aid to those who live in the outer areas of Iraq. Military trucks filled with mail, PX supplies, and other equipment for the Marines and Soldiers in FOBs in the area as well.

When I think of a road trip, I think of soft music playing on the radio and chatting with friends on the cell phone to help pass the time. I usually pack snacks and lunch, and only stop for gas and bathroom breaks. A convoy ride across the desert in Iraq is nothing like I just described. They are long and boring. They are not only noisy, but also intense. Traveling across the open desert in Iraq makes a convoy a sitting duck at times, not to mention other dangers like roadside bombs, and the possibility of breaking down in the middle of the desert. Let us not forget, I was stuck in a vehicle with no legroom. The seats were rock hard and killed both my back and my butt – oh, how I longed for first class. I stand five-foot eight inches, while most of the others were well over six foot and a lot bigger than I; throw in wearing body armor, and you can just imagine how uncomfortable I was during this convoy ride. Even though I drank a tremendous amount of water, during the nine and a half hour trip, bathroom breaks did not even come into my thoughts. I was more interested in getting from point A to point B as fast as we possibly could without any incidents.

Because the trip had been uneventful, it gave me time to think. What is out here that is so important to those who live here? There is only sand, sand and more sand. Along the way, I longed to see a tree, or even a lake, yet, all I could see was nothing but sand and dust. The heat was either getting to me, or pure boredom at one point, because for some strange reason, scenes from "Lawrence of Arabia" and "The Thief of Baghdad" popped into my thoughts. My mind wandered to characters traipsing across the desert on horseback and camels, fighting over treasures, princesses and land ownership. The radio came to life; I snapped back to reality because an IED was up ahead. My heart skipped a beat, while I hoped that maybe I had heard the announcement incorrectly, I looked over at Tony and he began looking out the window too. Just then, I noticed a sandbag on the side of the road, and there were wires sticking out of it. My heart sank, and I began to pray very hard that it did not go off while the convoy was driving past.

CHAPTER 16
LIFE IN A COMBAT ZONE

Thanks to Maryland's Army National Guard, we arrived safely at our destination. I was not only relieved, but also finally able to relax. I thanked the Captain and the rest of the group for getting us there safely, while Tony secured our gear.

The FOB was not what I expected it to be. I am not sure what I expected when I got here, but it was not as bad as I thought it was going to be. Do not get me wrong, it was still hot, sandy and dusty, but we had sturdy buildings and troop sleeping quarters called SWA-Huts. "SWA-Hut" was the name given to temporary wooden buildings, which are similar to sleeping bays used during the previous Gulf War. This is what the warriors would call home for as long as we were in Iraq. Unlike Camp Ripper, there were no tents or metal cans to house these warriors.

The forgotten warriors of this war are the Marines of the Al Anbar Province. This is probably because they do not complain, and are rarely mentioned in the media, unless there have been casualties. Media rarely comes out this way because this area is the real deal. It does not have the hotels of Baghdad, or the high concentration of combat activity that Fallujah, Ramadi, and Tikrit have. To the media there is no news here – there are no "if it bleeds, it leads" stories for them to exploit. Yet, there is something else out here – success. The Marines who patrol the area have the area secured.

Mind you, I was not expecting the Ritz Carlton, but conditions in this area were dismal. Nevertheless, the morale of the Marines was extremely high. Many of the Marines had been here before; they knew the area plus what to expect. One of the objectives of this trip was to experience a Transfer of Authority, better known as a TOA. Luckily, we arrived just in time to see it in full action. The outgoing leadership was extremely tense as they finalized their mission and began the long process of going home. It was evident that they were tired and drained from their deployment, yet they were very eager to brief the new leadership of forcible threats.

During the first 24 hours of my arrival, life was hectic. As the only female among so many Marines, I knew it would be a hardship during this time, but I went with the flow. As I said previously, I did not want to be a burden to these Marines, nor did I want any special treatment when it came to accommodations. Tony stayed with the Captain and First Sergeant in the main area of the base, while I was housed way on the other side in one of the vacant SWA-huts. It did not bother me because it was quiet and I would be able to write in the evenings. I felt safe once I realized the security dogs and their handlers were in the building next door.

Patrick, an Air Force Reservist, and his beautiful German Sheppard were great to hang out with after I settled in. At first, the dog did not come near me, but then I figured out his secret, and I was in like flint. He actually allowed me to pet him for a bit, plays with him while Patrick and I discussed the area and his time in Iraq. The hair on the dog's neck stood up and I backed away quickly. It turned out one of the Iraqi soldiers walked by; apparently, the dog did not trust him. Once I realized there were Iraqi soldiers on the base, my awareness levels sharpened.

Surrounding each of the SWA-Huts were Hescos. Hescos are mesh circles filled with sand to protect the structures and their inhabitants from any incoming rounds. They also provide areas for people to filter between buildings undetected. The first night alone in the SWA-Hut, I locked the doors from the inside. It was just after 9:30 in the evening when I heard voices, then doorknobs jiggled with fury, and I heard Arabic voices along the side of the building, then nothing. I sat up and reached for something in of my suitcase to use to defend myself should they gain access to my building. Thank God, it was not needed. There was no more movement outside, and I finally was able to go to sleep.

At chow (breakfast) the next morning, the Commanding Officer, Lt. Colonel Jones, and Sgt. Major Hatfield came by to say hello; they asked if I had slept well the night before. After an exchange of pleasantries, I advised them of the details to my evening's excitement. They were concerned and asked if I was okay. I explained what had happened and that I was quite prepared to defend myself if someone had entered my building. With a puzzled look upon their faces, I went on to say that I sat on my cot holding both my K-Bar (military style knife) and my Leatherman (utility knife), and was prepared to field dress anyone who entered my building. (Field dress - hunting term used to gut a deer) Although they laughed at my gut reaction to defend myself, I could see the concern on both their faces. Lt. Colonel Jones looked at his watch, and they both excused themselves. A short time later as I finished my breakfast, Lt. Colonel Jones came back and informed me I was to have my gear ready to be moved by 1500 (3 p.m.). I was puzzled, because I knew there was nothing available in the main area of the base, and said I would be fine where I was. He would not hear of it, I was to be ready to move that afternoon. It turned out a couple of Iraqi soldiers had broken a few locks along the row of buildings near where I was and had stolen items belonging to a few of the Marines. Lt. Colonel Jones did not want me harmed and made the decision to move the Major out of the VIP quarters while I was with them. The Transfer of Authority had not been finished as of yet and the Major had been housed in the VIP Quarters until he could move into his permanent quarters. I felt bad about displacing the Major and protested, but to no avail. I later learned that there were sleeping quarters affixed to each of the offices in the main building where the Major would be able to sleep comfortably, so I conceded.

Promptly at 1500, Lt. Pryor arrived with the Gator (a motorized golf-style cart) and we moved my gear into my new quarters. After the TOA was completed and everyone settled into their new quarters, the building I was moving into would become the visiting quarters for VIPs and guests. It was also a SWA-Hut, but this one had three mini-rooms with walls and a larger room on the other side where the Air Officer lived. This would be my home until I left Iraq. I settled in quickly and began to concentrate on my mission objectives.

Without any fanfare whatsoever, the transfer was over and the new patrols set up their rotations. Without skipping a beat, this new unit continued the protection of the area. Lt. Colonel Jones invited me to join him on his first patrol the next morning. I accepted.

Later that night, after observing the outgoing Chaplain's exit briefing in the Chapel, Tony and First Sergeant Gall appeared at the door and motioned for me to join them outside. Excited, Tony informed me there was a Civil Affairs Unit on base, and they were going out on a humanitarian mission the next morning. He said, "The Major in charge of the unit would be honored to accept us if you said 'yes.'" At first, I wasn't sure if should agree because I didn't want to insult Lt. Colonel Jones by changing plans just after I had agreed to join his patrol. I shared my concerns with both of them and First Sergeant Gall advised me that Lt. Colonel Jones knew of the humanitarian mission and was cool with it. So, of course, I said, "Yes." This was one of my objectives, to observe humanitarian missions so I could see firsthand the compassion of an American warrior. First Sergeant Gall offered to let Captain Puttroff know we'd be coming along in the morning. I had to go see the Major in charge of the Civil Affair Group and familiarize myself with the upcoming mission. I was excited.

When I returned to the hooch (military slang for sleeping quarters), I met up with Lt. Colonel Jones and confirmed that he knew of the changes. He was not only agreeable, he offered to show me where the CAG office was and introduce me to Major Don Caporale. The CAG Office was actually right next door to the VIP Quarters, but in the blackness of night, I did not notice the building.

The Lt. Colonel and I entered the CAG Office and met Major Caporale. After Lt Colonel Jones left, we began discussing my objectives and the mission for the next morning. The Major, a tall good-looking man in his early fifties, was excited that a writer was willing to accompany his unit on one of their missions. He introduced me to his team one by one:

Corporal Michael Kissiah, Corporal Charlie Carter, Sergeant Guillaume Plante, and Staff Sergeant Micotto. All were in their mid-twenties to early thirties. While I was in their office, I began to understand the missions they had been working on throughout the region. After the briefing, we hung out for a few hours laughing and swapping stories about the military. I felt at home around these Marines right from the beginning, never realizing how important they would become to me over the next few weeks. During one of our conversations, I mentioned that my two brothers were Marines and mentioned both their names. Major Caporale's mouth dropped on the floor and he started laughing. He and one of my brothers not only served together, but also were roommates during one of their tours together. Talk about divine intervention, he not only took me under his wing, but helped educate me on what it was to be in the CAG in a combat zone. I was in heaven.

The next morning we gathered at the staging area just after chow and began loading into vehicles for our first patrol. Tony and I rode in the back of what they call an LAV - Light Armor Vehicle. I will not describe the inside of this vehicle for obvious security reasons. Trust me when I say this – this vehicle was not built for comfort. We rolled out just after dawn and began our journey across the desert. The CAG was driving in Humvees which were filled with toys, blankets, and other supplies for the children and civilians of the area to which we were headed.

While on patrol with this one Civil Affairs Unit, I had the opportunity to interact with and observe a few of the villages where they had been working. I could envision the Civil Affairs Marine's glamorous life in a combat zone, but to see it conducted in person was something very different. To see the faces of citizens running up to these warriors with open arms and bright smiles is not what I would have expected in that situation. The look upon the faces of the children who received toys, or even bottles of fresh water, was both heartwarming and heartbreaking at the same time.

During our journey, we visited many locations, all of which showed serious signs of being at far less than we would think of as poverty levels. One such village consisted of single-story row houses, or apartments, built of brick, concrete and clay. Each dwelling was home to three or four families. Litter lined the streets, along with pieces of broken buildings and glass. Although each home had sanitation means, they were nonfunctional. With no running water or electricity to work these systems, the inhabitants would use either the roof or the backyard to defecate among the animals. Those animals in most cases would become the food for future meals. The smell could be overwhelming at times, and I could only imagine what it would smell like in the heat of summer.

Children played in the streets and alleyways amid the barbed wire, as this is now normal to them. To see this type of devastation and poverty was hard to comprehend. Granted we have poverty at home, but at least we have the amenities of basic decent living conditions and do not allow our children to play amid dangerous barbed wire.

To observe how the people of Iraq lived, under the control of the former government, can turn your stomach.

Even so, there were successes all around the area, some small, some huge. Someone not from the area might not think so, but to the locals the successes were abundant, for example, the functioning water treatment plant along the Euphrates River. We learned from the locals that this plant, built back in the 70s before the leadership of Saddam Hussein to service a large area of Iraq, hadn't been maintained properly since Hussein had come into power. It was to have serviced a large area of Iraq, so was a serious hardship to the locals. The plant, which had once produced running water and electricity, became dormant under his leadership in order to maintain control over the people in the area. One must understand this man's mindset. He was an oppressor; by instilling fear in the people of Iraq, he had them at his mercy. When he shut down the water plant, he was then able to control them. They became dependent upon him for everything, from food, water, to necessities of life. Meanwhile, he lived in complete luxury in palaces, built by the people he oppressed. In each of his palaces, which were elaborate to say the least, he not only had the basics of living, but also the best that money could buy. Money earned by the people of Iraq was bleed from each of them under his leadership due to his exorbitant prices for the necessities of life.

Although the climate in the United States is much more temperate, most American's take air conditioning for granted. In Iraq, where the temperature can reach as high as 140 degrees, an air conditioner under Saddam's leadership came at a premium. We learned that air conditioners or air coolers had cost approximately $1,000 under his control. The price of these same units dropped drastically, to around $200, after the coalition forces took over the country. They are not merely a luxury to these people, but nearly a necessity of life. Still, there are areas where the poverty levels are so low that families cannot afford them. With limited electricity in most areas, the people of Iraq are unable to use their cooling systems throughout the day. Where there is no electricity, the United State military has brought in generators, to run for a few hours each day in order to take the edge off the hottest part of each day.

I was lucky to have received the assistance of the unit's translator, while we were in the villages. The Marines call him Mike. Mike, an Iraqi citizen works with coalition forces as a liaison and translator for both the Iraqi's and Coalition Forces. He is one of many throughout the country who have sacrificed the love and support of their family to help make a difference for their people and country. As of March of 2006, Mike had not seen his wife and children for over two years.

One evening, I had the opportunity of having an in-depth conversation with Mike about his involvement with Coalition Forces. He relayed the many concerns his people had at first when American Forces landed in his country. "Will they occupy our country and treat us just as bad as Hussein treated us all these years?" "Will they oppress us in the same way and use us as test subjects for their crazy experiments?" "Will they hold our land and our legacy hostage as he did?" One major concern he relayed was how Saddam Hussein came into village after village and took away the land that once belonged to families for generations. He killed the elders and replaced them with his loyal henchman. Within a matter of minutes of taking over the village, villagers lost everything they owned, land, animals, and luxuries. The henchman put in charge treated them like slaves and animals. They could not walk down the street without fear of death or kidnapped - never to return and see their families again. "There are thousands of people who vanished under his control; their bodies never found." He said. "My uncle was one of those people," he added with his head hung down remembering the last time he saw him. I felt for his loss and now understood why he felt compelled to work with the Coalition to rid his country of this terrible evil.

In order to understand what he was telling me, I asked him a few strategic, yet delicate questions: "There are many uprisings of violence throughout the country, are they insurgent driven, religious driven or something else?" and, "If your people are so happy that none of this happened, why is there so many uprising throughout the country?" I asked him. "Many of the uprisings are not because the Americans are here. They are internal frustrations of people wanting what once belonged to them back. They want the land that belonged to their families for generations, and family items stolen by Saddam's men returned to them. Now that Saddam is gone, they are empowered to reclaim what once belonged to them." He replied. "Those of us who are intelligent know it is not about religion. We have Sunni, Shia and Kurds working side by side and together with the Coalition to help combat the insurgents. Many of the insurgents want to help fuel the fire of hatred among my people. They are left over's from Saddam's Regime who have joined forces with the terrorists of other countries to undermine what the coalition is trying to accomplish for my people." He said.

I sat back and tried to understand, and then it hit me – Hatfield and McCoy legend. One took land from the other and the feud continued for years. Troublemakers had taken sides with one another and helped fuel the feud along the way. Now I understood what was happening in his country.

"So what you are saying is this for example: I owned land and Saddam came into my village and took it away from me and gave it to you. Now that he is gone I am going to fight to the death with you to reclaim what once belonged to me, but you are now set in your ways and will not give it back, right?" I said. "Exactly" he said.

"Should it be considered a civil war or something else?" I asked. "It is not a civil war by any means; it is simply taking back what once belonged to a family for a thousand years." He replied.

I wanted to understand the religious aspect of this situation and began asking many questions. Mike knew I was interested in understanding his culture and he was more than happy to help me understand.

I began with, "Mike, so that I understand the difference, please explain the between the Sunni, Shia or Shiite and Kurds?"

He began with the Kurds in the North. "The Kurds are considered a tribe in the northern area of the country, a nomad mountain tribe that is a mixture of Iraqi, Iranian, Turkish, and Syrians. They are also a mixture of Shia and Sunni Muslims. The Sunni's would be closely equal to your Protestant religion, while the Shia or Shiite is considered the higher religion of the Muslim faith. Shia in the Muslim faith would be the same as what the Catholic Church is to the Christian faith. Throughout history there has always been a strain between the Shia and Sunni faiths as to who is the direct descendent from Mohammad." When he was finished, I had a better understanding of who each were, finally. The strain reminds me of the Protestant versus Catholic wars of Europe and Northern Ireland.

The next day we went out on patrol into one of the villages, and someone asked Mike who I was. He told them I was a journalist from America. Many began saying how grateful they were to the American Forces for helping them against the insurgents and for getting rid of the tyrant Saddam Hussein. Through the interrupter, one woman said, although their home had a toilet, she had never seen it in operation. "She was like a kid with a new toy when the Marines fixed it for her; she kept flushing and flushing," her husband said, smiling broadly. Then he pulled out a Polaroid picture, which showed him and his wife each holding their index fingers in the air. Because I did not speak Arabic, I turned to our translator for help once again. "It is a picture of them voting for the first time," he said. Just then, the man began speaking quickly, and the translator tried to keep up, "Thank you, thank you, thank you. For the first time in my life, I feel I am finally free. When he was removed, I did not feel it at first, but when I voted for the first time," he said as his smile got brighter and his eyes welled up with tears, "I knew what freedom felt like. I am in control now. Please thank the Americans for giving me the opportunity to know what freedom feels like." Tears began to well up in my eyes at hearing what this man had to say. His wife standing close by was also smiling and she too had tears in her eyes.

The locals are not fully aware of the sacrifices and dedication of the men who repaired their local water treatment plant near the Euphrates River. They know it was the American forces that gave them water, but still, they do not know who to thank. One woman begged that I relay her thanks and appreciation to those who gave her running water. I promised I would. Because of the work performed by the Marines and the Navy Seabees, not only do the people of Al Anbar have running water now, but they also have electricity.

In some of the outer areas of Iraq, many people still do not have running water due to blockages in the water lines. The coalition forces, however, deliver bottled water, or bring trucks filled with water, on a weekly basis for many of these towns. One of the missions I accompanied these Marines on was a mission of this type. The convoy contained provisions for the people in the outer areas of this province. Simple luxuries that you and I take for granted each day, are lifesaving for these people. Please remember this the next time you open a bottle of water.

Throughout this trip, I had three unique experiences that those in the media never get, much less a female. I was able to sit in on three strategic meetings with former insurgents who are now working with the Coalition Forces. As a writer, I was thrilled to have these experiences; but I knew as a woman, it was unheard of. In the culture of this region, women are not included in business meetings at all let alone something as sensitive. I knew I was observing a unique meeting and was excited to ask questions at the end. I was eager to learn what changed their minds about allowing me to attend.

After one such meeting, the first man admitted to working with insurgents in the past, but had began working with coalition forces to help combat his former comrades. I could not resist asking him what caused him to side with the American and Coalition Forces. When our translator began to speak, I looked deep into this man's eyes searching his soul so as to understand if he was telling the truth or not. "While I was somewhere else planning an attack against American Forces in the North, the insurgents attacked our village and tried to kill our families. They were the same people I was working with, but the Marines saved our families. That is when I realized the insurgents did not care about us, as a people. They were not fighting for Iraq or its people; they just wanted to kill people. That is when I knew I was working against my own people, my own family, and my own history. I did not want to be considered a martyr for death, but for life," he said. He seemed sincere in his words and his body language. The hatred I detected in his eyes for his former friends seemed genuine. I am not sure why I believed him, but his actions spoke louder than words. During his meeting with the Marines, he handed over a folder that contained a list of sixty-seven names of insurgents and where they could be located.

After walking away from this group, another local man came running up. The Marines surrounded me like a security blanket, but allowed the man to speak. He pointed to a man on crutches, and I began walking towards him with Mike in tow. All the while, the Marines did not allow me to venture far from their side. I looked down at the man's foot and asked Mike to find out what happened to him. As he began to speak in Arabic, I looked into the eyes of the injured man standing before me and listened intently at his reply. "I injured my leg and foot during an attack and I thought I would bleed to death, but the Americans," he pointed to the Marines who were standing around us, "They sent me to a doctor, he fixed my leg and saved my life." He said with a trembling voice. I was not sure what he meant so I asked, "Was he injured in a battle, or just fell down?" His reply was direct and stern. "We were attacked by those crazy men, but they saved us, they saved my life," he said as he pointed at the Marines again. "Insurgents were attacking their village and the Marines were on patrol nearby and heard the shooting. They came to help the people of his village fight them off," the translator said. The man's smile said it all, he was grateful to Coalition Forces for coming to his aid. I watched the man for a while from a distance as he looked out over the sea of Marines in the courtyard, the smile on his face said he was glad they were in his village.

Before we left the village, one local man asked to have his picture taken with me. I thought nothing of it and handed my camera to the Captain. I stood next to this Iraqi man and he put his arm around my back, and then he grabbed my ass. I was in shock. I walked away briskly while telling Tony and the Captain that he had just grabbed my ass. The Captain handed me my camera, Tony walked over to the man, and said to take his picture too, and so I did. I am not sure what happened, or if Tony said anything, but when I lowered the camera, the man looked at me and then at Tony and at hurried away fast. As a bodyguard, Tony was great to have around to take care of situations like this. When I asked Tony what he said to the man, he just shrugged and gave me a Cheshire grin. I knew not to ask any more questions after that. He earned his paycheck as far as I was concerned.

As I listened to the villagers speak of how life had changed for the better, because of our brave warriors, I found myself grasping for words of acknowledgement. I felt a mixture of sadness and pain for the way they lived, but an overwhelming sense of pride soon took over my emotions; it was my fellow Americans, who helped these people regain their dignity and self worth. When we left the area and began our journey back to the FOB, all I could think about was why our media has not reporting these kinds of stories to the American people in their news reports? What is making them hold back such wonderful stories? What motive could they possibly have to keep these stories hidden from the public? These and many other questions flooded my mind as we drove through the desert.

Showers

After returning from our patrol, the only thing I wanted was a long hot shower, but unfortunately, I was in the desert surrounded by Marines and Iraqi Soldiers. The base was equipped with a shower tent, which is for the men. This realization caused me to appreciate my time in both Kuwait and Camp Ripper, because they both had facilities for both males and females to take showers. I kept reminding myself that I had a unique opportunity at this FOB, and would not complain about any inconvenience I might have. Although I longed for a real shower, according to the schedule, the only time I would be allowed to take a shower would be either 2230 (10:30 p.m.) or before 0600 (6:00 a.m.) in the morning. Even though the tent was not far from my Hooch, I still would have had to walk through the blackness of night and be vulnerable in the shower tent. Knowing that there was a female on post, I noticed the Iraqi soldiers were hanging around excessively near where I was living. Not being able to see them in the dark, lurking around, I took no chances. Instead of complaining, I got creative and accustomed to taking field showers for the duration of my stay in this area. This consisted of using four to six large bottles of water to wash both hair and body each day. Thank heaven for those Hescos that surrounded the building, and the blackness of night.

Over the course of the next few weeks, I realized I had it easy in the FOB. Marines stationed in the outer areas of this region had it much worse. They lived like nomads in the desert, stuck in makeshift posts surrounded by sandbags, without the luxuries of chow halls, shower tents, or even port-a-potties. Therefore, I did not complain about the lifestyle in which I was living; I just rolled with it. It was all part of the experience of living alongside those in uniform for a short time. Life is very interesting in a combat zone, so I could not complain; at least I was alive.

For the next few weeks, we went out on various patrols, which gave me an opportunity to observe our Marines at their best. While on one patrol, we came upon one of those mini-posts and my heart sank when I saw how these Marines were living. It was way out in the desert on the outskirts of a village. Surrounded by sandbags, it was hot and dusty with no shade for relief.

As I stood talking to a few of the Marines, Tony approached and said I had to see something. We walked a few yards and I about fell on the ground laughing. He was pointing to a makeshift wooden port-a-john with three stalls, each having a toilet seat and nothing else. I can remember laughing that out of all the FOBs we had entered, this shit-hole of a post had actual toilet paper; but where were the base workings of the toilet? I came to find out that they do not use cans or buckets; they use black plastic bags for their waste. In all the other locations, we used wet-ones when using the port-a-potties, but they had real toilet paper. Go figure. The real funny part of this trip was that before I entered Iraq, you would never have caught me using a port-a-john anywhere in the U.S. – not for any amount of money in the world. After living in this environment, even for a short time, port-a-johns are not a problem for me anymore – just as long as I have my trusty wet-ones.

I watched the Marines interacting with locals who were happy to see them. While they inspected various projects, I watched as they discussed plans for the project. Even though the females in their culture are never involved in business transactions, I was honored to be allowed to stay and observe. They made this concession because I am an American journalist and one they were told was there to tell what the media usually omits from nightly American broadcasts. I discovered these meetings were no different from any negotiations back home - each side expressing their needs and offering an exchange of mutual ideas and strategies to achieve common goals of success. Even though they wanted to make an effort for success in their project, all the while in the pit of my stomach I did not trust them. Although they seemed sincere in their efforts, be it loyalty to the Marines or just a gut feeling, I felt as though they were just taking what they could until we left. Were they allowing us to pay for repairs of the infrastructures that Saddam never paid for?

During one of the last meetings I attended before I left the country, I encountered one man who gave me a message for the American people. Having once been a General in Saddam's Army and disagreed with many of Hussein objectives and tactics, he found himself ostracized and fled the country for his own safety. With great sacrifice and dedication to the new cause, he returned to Iraq in order to offer his assistance to the Coalition Forces after the removal of Saddam from power.

He was a jovial man in his mid fifties with a pleasant demeanor. One Marine, Corporal Plante, had become his favorite while working with this group of Marines. Knowing it would be the last time they would see each other, the General seemed saddened that he would not continue not to see his new friend and presented him with a parting gift. His gift was an Iraqi scarf to remember him. Corporal Plante was not the only one to receive a gift; the General presented us all with a similar scarf as his way of thanking the group for their assistance to his village and his country.

In this culture, it is customary for each party to inquire as to the well-being of the others family members, children, and parents and then spouse while they waited for Chai tea to be served. It is also customary to share a meal during business meetings, but time did not afford us that luxury during this meeting. As the meeting went on, they discussed the progress of specific projects and goals for future projects. Since this group of Marines would be leaving shortly, they introduced their replacements to the General. In an effort to ensure the General that, this new group of Marines was up to speed, they discussed all pending projects and agreements.

After the meeting was over, I was able to ask the General a few questions. My first question was, "Why was he working with the Marines and Coalition Forces?" and my second was, "Why did he feel it was important for us to be there?" To be clear and not lost in translation, he replied straightforwardly, and in his broken English said, "That bastard is gone and we must rebuild our country. Your government is helping us to rebuild after many years of oppression by a mad man. Please tell to your people, we are truly happy that you helped us regain our country. Be sure to tell them, great things are happening here because of your soldiers. Thanks to their help, we will be able to rebuild Iraq for its people and leave a better country for our children to live in. It will take time, but we have a good start thanks to Americans like these men who help us every day become stronger so we might be able to stand on our own two feet and be proud once again." As we said our good-byes, the General took my hand in his and held it very gently, wishing me well and safe passage on my journey. His parting words are still with me to this day - "Do not be like those others and tell our story falsely. Tell the truth of what you have seen here, because God is watching and only he knows the truth of what is happening in this country. He knows the evil is still lurking in the hearts of those who were allies to that mad man."

When I walked away from the General, a few of the Marines asked what he had to say to me, but I could not reply for some reason. I was not sure if it was a message or a warning at that point. As we walked back to the vehicles from his building, the Marines surrounded me just as they had done on previous patrols. The feeling was that they were even more vigilant in this instance.

As I began shaping my journal entries into this story, the greater understanding of the Generals words began to seep in. There is an evil plaguing their country, and the observers who are not telling the truth of what is happening in Iraq are only adding to that evil. One has to wonder why this is happening. Is it individuals who refuse to report the accomplishments achieved in that country, or is political gain, personal profit, or malice that drives them? On the other hand, is it because of political jealousy that they refuse to report the truth? Is the truth not always better then fiction?

Good-byes have never been easy for me, and the circumstances surrounding this trip made any good-bye that much more difficult. It was the evening before I left the FOB when it hit me, I could not say good-bye to these warriors. I had just finished the last short briefing, standing by, waiting for First Sergeant Gall to finish speaking to his Platoon Leaders when it hit me. Unscripted he turned to me and asked if I had anything to say to the guys before he dismissed them. I am usually never lost for words, but in that moment, I had a very hard time speaking. The words began to leave my lips and I felt my throat closing up. The only words I could muster were to ask them to relay my thanks to their fellow Marines for the honor and privilege of spending time with them. As the last word left my lips, I had to turn and walk away fast. The emotions, which rose up in me as I was leaving these warriors, hit me hard. I realized the bond I now had with these Marines, would not allow me to say good-bye to them without being reduced to tears. Oh, hell no, I would not let them see me in such a weak state of mind, with tears coming from the hardnosed female who had been toughing it out all those weeks. But in those last few moments, as I looked at their faces standing there before me, I realized I now looked upon these warriors as my adopted sons, and my heart was breaking that I could not bring them home with me and keep them safe. As I walked away, my eyes began to well up with tears, and I began begging God to watch over them for me, because they had kept me safe from harm while I was with them. The most difficult thing I have ever done was to leave them behind and not bring them home with me.

Before Returning to Civilization

The last place we stayed was called "Korean Village" FOB. The story behind the name of this fob is one that depicts the true essence of how Saddam conducted his business throughout the country. His objective was to build as much as he could on the backs of the local people. Because of the extremely remote location, Korean Village received its name from the Korean construction workers who were hired to build the highway between Baghdad and the western borders of Iraq. The workers refused to live in tents so far out in the open desert they constructed a community as their own little oasis. Because Saddam never paid the Korean's, they abandoned their village and Coalition forces later discovered it. What a pleasant surprise for the coalition not to have to build from scratch in such a remote area.

It was in this quaint village where I finally found a chow hall where I could relax and enjoy a meal. The atmosphere was the best of all; I guess you could say they saved the best for last. The reason for my comfort was not only that this chow hall was an old style eating facility run by a great group of real Marines, not locals. It was bright and cheery, with colorful artwork lining the interior walls. Each piece of artwork told the story of each unit that has served the FOB since American Forces arrived. The food was the same style as in other Fobs', but seemed to taste better. Maybe it was because the nine Marines of the Air Wing from Camp Pendleton, California, took their jobs seriously, as they prepared the food. These individuals fed us breakfast and dinner meals each day because we were out on patrol midday. The staff saved us from having to eat MREs (Meals Ready to Eat) a number of times by staying late to feed us a hot meal when we returned late at night from patrols. After being in a convoy for 16 hours, we were all famished and really needed a good home-cooked meal. One cannot complain about real food cooked over an open pit, by people who respect you for who you are and what you do. This of all the chow halls we had the pleasure of dining in, was the best.

CH53 Trip

I promised to tell the truth in this book, and that is exactly what I plan to do, even though it might include an embarrassing moment for me.

After breakfast, Tony and I decided to make our lives easier. We packed up our excess gear, keeping only what we thought we would need for the next three days with us. By this point, we realized it was easier to just mail everything home, rather than carry it back on the last leg of our trip. I would come to realize that packing one essential item was a big mistake.

Tony and I arrived at the airfield later that morning to await the chopper that would take us back to Camp Ripper. While waiting, I enjoyed a last-minute cup of coffee with the Air

Officer. I asked him questions about protocols for the ride and he gave me some good advice. If I felt sick, I was to remove my helmet and use it as a barf bag. That was good; the only problem was that I would have to clean it out once I got to Ripper. I could deal with that for sure.

The Chopper arrived and we boarded along with everyone else. This was where I made the biggest mistake of my life – I locked up once I sat down. This was the first and only time during the trip that I was scared out of my skin. We took off, and the combination of smelling the aviation fuel, the heat and the combat maneuver movement of the chopper made me extremely queasy. I began to overheat and felt my stomach doing flip-flops. Just then, I unhooked the strap to my helmet and flipped it off my head. I could not move my head in either direction for fear of losing the contents of my stomach. Embarrassment about being sick began to make things worse for me. The person sitting to my left knocked my helmet out of my hands and I about lost it, but could not move or even say a word. I was frantic. No one would have been able to hear me, even if I were able to say anything, because of all the noise of the chopper. Out of nowhere, a clear plastic bag appeared under my chin – "thank God for small favors," I thought – and then it happened, I began losing the contents of my breakfast for the rest of the trip. I was so embarrassed it was not funny. My backpack was right in front of me, but I could not move to grab the wet-ones from the pouch. As if he was reading my mind, I felt Tony tapping my leg, he was handing me his.

When I lifted my head for a brief moment, I looked over at the Gunner. He motioned with a thumb up and smiled at me. I returned a half-hearted smile because it was all I could muster. I could not look at anyone else onboard because I was so embarrassed. We made one stop along the way, and I was able to feel the earth for a bit. I thought my queasy stomach problems were over, but something told me not to let go of the bag. We were up in the air once again, and it happened again. "Damn, there was nothing left in my stomach; what is wrong with me?" I thought. I felt as though I just wanted to jump out the back hatch, but I could not move. Besides, if God wanted me to fly he would have given me wings, right? By the time we landed back at Al Asad, I could not look at anyone who was on board with us. I walked away from that chopper like a wounded puppy with my head dangling down with such embarrassment and shame. Now mind you, I had brought both Dramamine and Bonine with me for this one purpose; unfortunately, I packed it in the box that I had just shipped home that morning. Stupid me for not thinking ahead, but who knew?

While we waited for the driver to come pick us up, I tried to sip on a bit of warm Coke to help settle my stomach. In front of the terminal stood a group of people who kept trying to get me to take a piece of gum, but I could not think of putting anything near my lips except the stale Coke. An officer walked up, stood right in front of me, and said, "Ma'am, we're all pilots. We know how you're feeling right now, and trust us when we say, Chew on a piece of gum. It will help settle your stomach." I looked up at him and he was not smiling; but the look in his eyes told me he had been there a few times himself. I took the gum and began chewing it slowly. One of the other officers made a quick comment. "Her color is coming back, she'll be okay now." The officer who gave me the gum walked back over to me and put his hands on my shoulders. "Oh yeah, and by the way, Ma'am, welcome to the CH53 Club! You've now been christened!" He said as he gave me a sisterly shoulder squeeze. They all laughed and said they had been there once or twice themselves. I did not feel embarrassed anymore after talking to them. Apparently, everyone gets sick on those damn contraptions at least once in their lifetime in a combat zone. Welcome to the CH53 Club, my foot! As worried as I was about taking a convoy in the beginning of this journey, after my experience on the CH53, a convoy was much more appealing.

Staff Sergeant Griffith, who was one of our Public Affairs liaisons at Camp Ripper, arrived to pick us up. After taking one look at me, he knew I had tossed my cookies in the chopper. Although I knew he wanted to laugh, he did not. We drove over to Ripper's side of the base and unloaded our gear into the same Can I was in before. Tony stopped off at the tents to settle in for the evening.

I was grateful to be back at Camp Ripper where they had both male and female showers. Knowing I could take a long overdue shower, it did not take me long to get my gear together and head to those shower fast. Although I can usually take a complete shower within less than seven minutes, I relished being under the water for over forty. I felt guilty for using so much water, but I figured I had saved so much water in the last few weeks; I was entitled to a long one.

Later that evening we had a brief meeting with the Commanding Officer for the Area of Operations of Al Anbar area. We gave our grateful thanks for the opportunity to visit his Marines and I retired for the evening. After chow the next morning, we were off and running once again – this time en route to Kuwait on our way home.

CHAPTER 17
COMPASSION FOR AN AMERICAN WARRIOR

"Virtues," are opinions, beliefs, and ideas of any given subject. These virtues are what make up a person's core value system that they live by on a daily basis. A person's individual values help them to conduct themselves in society according to their beliefs (integrity, honor, morality, loyalty, generosity, compassion, sacrifice). Each of these values is what makes up the character of a person.

The word "Compassion" as defined in the dictionary is "the sympathetic consciousness of others' distress together with a desire to alleviate it."

In today's society, the word compassion is not a virtue; it is considered interference in our lives.

When people think of a combat zone, they think of death and destruction of human life and property. Instead, they should think of the word compassion, for it is everywhere, especially in the hearts and minds of the American Warriors.

I was amazed at how many times the word compassion came to mind as I watched the way our military forces interacted with the Iraqi people. They were not the "bloodthirsty mongers the media portrayed them as," on the contrary, they were genuinely patient, helpful and most of all passionate in helping the people they were there to protect.

The most gratifying moment for any Marine in this area is when they helped members of a Sunni tribe, living in tents in the middle of the desert. They arrived to provide them with food, water, medical assistance, and blankets. "You would have thought I gave them a million dollars, the way they reacted. It was just a few bottles of water and a blanket." Cpl Charles Carter said. "They were so grateful; one woman was reduced to tears, clutching the items to her chest as if they were made of gold." He added. "I have never seen anyone so grateful for insignificant items like that before." He said looking off into the desert. The smile that came to his face said it all. It grew bigger and brighter the more he thought of the people he helped.

While on patrol, Cpl Michael Kassiah handed a child a few of his MRE's and the child ran away smiling, clutching them to his chest. The Marines were all smiles knowing they had just given his family a meal for that evening. A few minutes later, the same child returned with homemade bread and handed it to Kassiah. He did not want to take it, knowing they had very little food of their own, but in this culture, it would have been an insult not so he accepted the bread.

Corporal Plante of the Civil Affairs Unit relayed the story of a little girl who was running towards crossfire between insurgents as they drove into a village. She tripped and began screaming from pain; she had broken her leg. Risking his own life, he ran to her side, scooping her up in his arms and carried her to safety. When the helicopters landed a short time later to gather wounded, he handed her little body over to a Marine on the chopper, with instructions to have her leg looked after. The scared little five-year-old girl was taken care of by medical staff at a nearby unit. They looked after her as if she were one of their own children for the next few weeks. Plante drove back into the village a few weeks later. This was a special mission for him; to deliver a little girl wearing a pink cast on her leg, with a bright smile, back to her parents. That was his most memorable moment, he said, "Seeing the joy on the parents' faces as I placed her tiny body in her father's arms. Her mother cried with joy at seeing her little girl alive and well."

In Baghdad, Fallujah, Ramadi and other places throughout the country, there are thousands of similar stories of the same compassion. There are similar stories coming out of Afghanistan. A soldier with the 82nd Airborne relayed his memorable experience, delivering supplies to a newly opened school just north of Baghram.

"It was my first humanitarian assistance drop," Sergeant First Class Michael Rider said with a smile. "I will always remember that experience. We were in the mountains of

Afghanistan in December of 2002. It was cold and we drove four hours to get to the top of the mountain. There was an all girls' school that had just opened. We arrived with seven trucks filled with supplies. It was so cool, you know." He added. "We were overwhelmed with emotion when we saw how they had been living. To see the expression on their faces as we handed out supplies. They were just simple little things like pens, pencils, backpacks, paper, and blankets to help them weather the coldness of the mountains; but to them they were precious gifts. They were so grateful and happy for the assistance. It was so rewarding to have been a part of that mission. It is the most memorable memory I have of my tour in Afghanistan."

When we think of medical personnel, we think of only wounded soldiers hanging on for dear life. We never think of how many times medical personnel have gone out into a village to conduct medical examinations of men, women, and children suffering the same ailments as you and I do. The difference being the lack of medical assistance could be life threatening. The many hours they have endured past their normal shift to watch over a person who has a non-combat medical condition, like the flu or high fever. We do not think about the life saving surgeries they have performed that eased pain or saved a life. We never imagine the many times a doctor or a nurse has sat with a child who didn't understand where they were and feared their surroundings so they could recover more quickly.

Each day we carry on with our own lives and take for granted the little things that mean so much to others. We especially take for granted those of our Armed Forces who are sacrificing each day and who are performing such amazing acts of compassion to help others in our name.

I have asked many a warrior who has come home from Iraq, the same question, "Would you go back if given the chance?" Nine out of ten times, I receive the same response, with the same passion in their voice, "In a heartbeat." This is the same answer, I give to people when asked the same question, – "I would go back in a heartbeat if given the chance."

There is something very special about a human being who is sent to a combat zone with one mission in mind – destroy the enemy, but who comes home filled with pride rather than medals; they have made a difference in people's lives – one person at a time. I believe this is the reason why so many of our warriors come home changed. They have seen first hand, the power and compassion of their fellow Americans. For they have the virtues one can only aspire to have – honor, integrity, morality, loyalty, generosity, compassion and they are willing to sacrifice themselves in the name of freedom.

CHAPTER 18
JOURNEY HOME
BACK IN KUWAIT

The process for departing from a combat zone is a lot longer than it was going in. In our case, it would be longer than normal. Once we made it to Kuwait, it was the out-processing from hell.

In order to get onboard the plane heading back to California, we had to go through CFCLCC (Coalition Force Land Component Command) to obtain our orders. We arrived at the processing center at about 11 o'clock in the evening, and at that hour, there was a skeleton crew. Maybe it was the hour, or a lack of staffing, but no one seemed to know anything. Luckily, we found one person who knew his job exceptionally well. Within thirty minutes, we had new orders and sat for over an hour waiting on a ride to the Marine Corps side of the base. We were exhausted and caught a nap on the wooden benches in the holding area.

Finally, our ride appeared and we were off to our destination. It was almost 0230 (2:30 a.m.) when we arrived at the base from which we started. Only a month prior that area was buzzing like a hornet's nest, now it was like a ghost town; quiet and sparse. It took another 40 minutes to settle in, and by the time I hit the rack, I was out cold. This experience was nothing like the first time. This time I slept in the back of one of the females' tents, a tent that only housed six females stationed at the base. They were not as welcoming as the first set of females I bunked with.

Once in Kuwait we only had to wait one day before the long trip home. At this point, my mission was complete and I was ready to go home. As I walked around the once busy camp, I felt as though I had walked into a ghost town. The wind blew up sand and I thought of the old west town's that had long been abandoned and I half expected to see a tumbleweed roll by. Then I noticed many of the transient sleeping quarters were missing.

After gathering our gear, we joined the group of Marines we would be traveling home with, and the long journey home began. Wait; there was another hurry-up-and-wait situation – this time an extremely long wait once we finished getting through the security aspect. I will never complain about security at our airports ever again after this trip. We lugged our stuff from one security checkpoint to another, and each person inspected everyone's duffle bags and backpacks. At each checkpoint we were repeatedly asked the same group of questions, "Do you have any unused ammunition, weapons, vials of sand, or other items that you should not be taking out of the country?" then it was, "Do you have any lighters, matches, or other explosive materials in your possession?"

When we entered the last checkpoint, we were instructed to empty out our duffle bags and backpacks onto a counter for inspection. What I found quite odd was that all those around me had to go through this procedure, except me. The Navy representative who was my security guy only touched my bag and told me to move along. I looked at him and was shocked. I just stood on that line outside for an hour only to be told to move along. I not only found this to be odd, but concerning. I was a civilian, and I could have had anything in my bags.

I took my time walking out of the building and made a point of looking around at each security station in the room. One observation that I made was that those who were assigned to do this job were not only disrespectful to those leaving the country, but they were condescending to them as well, taking duffle bags and flipping them around until the entire contents were all over the place, then taking each piece and tossing it to the side. On many occasions, they were not even looking at the items at all, but smiling to their friends across the room. Here were Americans just coming out of a battle zone being treated like second-class citizens by fellow Americans.

After the long wait through security, we were herded like cattle through yet another maze to a new holding area where we were given Army style MREs, and sat on uncomfortable benches until it was time to leave for the plane.

This last holding pattern wasn't bad for me actually, because it gave me an opportunity to talk too many of the warriors I would be traveling home with. I asked many light questions, such as, "What will you do first when you get home?" The answer was always the same, "Sleep." Then I asked, "What the second thing you will do is and the third" The answer was always the same, "Raid the fridge, eat real food, and drink a case of beer." This last answer always came with a hearty laugh.

As the sun came up over the horizon, we began to line up for the trip to the plane. This queuing up also took some time. It was much easier to enter a combat zone than it was to leave one.

After getting on the plane, just about everyone fell asleep quickly. We arrived in Ireland for a short layover, which allowed me to leave the plane for a bit and breathe in some Irish air. Meanwhile, everyone else headed to the Guinness Bar that is always open at the airport for American service members. The gift shop across the way was also open, and I could not help but peruse its trinkets. Okay, yes, I bought two things while I was in there – come on, I am Irish – I had to buy something that was from Ireland - even if I was only in the air terminal.

The trip across the Atlantic felt as though it was taking forever, but then the pilot announced that we had entered into U.S. airspace and my heart skipped a beat – home. We stopped off in Bangor, Maine, once again, and this time the warm faces and smiles of Betty, John, Mildred, Beth and the others were like being welcomed home by family. When John saw me coming down the runway with Tony he about fell over with excitement. He wrapped his arms around me, gave me a kiss on the cheek, and immediately steered me to the door for a cigarette and a brief chat. After we returned upstairs, the rest came over to say hello and to hear my reports of my journey. It was like old home week, seeing these wonderful people once again. Unfortunately, our time with them was brief, and in what seemed to be a flash, we were off again.

When we touched down at March Air Force Base and loaded up the buses, I was relieved to be back. The drive back to Twenty-Nine Palms was the same as before we left, nothing had changed. Once on base, we called Lt. Borrero, and he sent someone to pick us up while the Marines unloaded their weapons at the Armory.

We arrived at the Welcome Home site where the families were waiting in earnest for their loved one's arrival. As we walked across the grass, an uptight female Marine stopped us and demanded to know who I was. After explaining that I just arrived home with the warriors who would be arriving in a short time, her first reaction was to inform me that I could not take any pictures of any of the families or the Marines coming off the bus. It turned out her best friend was standing next to her and she worked for a major newspaper. I didn't have to wonder why she said I could not take any pictures. Just then, Brigadier General Stone, the Commanding General of the base, walked by and noticed me standing there. Right in front of this female Marine, he came over, welcomed me home personally, and inquired about my experience with the Marines in Iraq. After giving him a quick "it was an awesome experience, Sir" reply, I could not help it; I looked over at the female Marine as I asked him for permission to take pictures of the Marines as they greeted their families. She was royally pissed off that I did this, but I was delighted because he said, "Yes." He added, with a big grin on his face, "You just came home with these guys; of course you can take pictures." Let her outrank his stars with a rebuttal I thought. A little while later, I discovered who she was and why she had such a problem with me. She was a member of the PAO group who had caused so many problems at the beginning of my trip. It occurred to me what type of reprimand she and the others received after my phone call back to Washington. Apparently, she was still at it, at least she was consistent.

As the Marines came off the bus, they were greeted with hugs and kisses from loved ones. I could not help but think of the Marines I had left behind in Iraq. I wondered the whole time how they were doing and if they were safe. When the festivities were over, we returned to the hotel and got some much-needed sleep.

The next day was a blur, I didn't realize how tired I was until I looked at the clock, and it was almost dinnertime. We had dinner with Lt. Borrero that evening and the next morning we were off to San Diego.

Once we arrived back in San Diego and checked into the hotel, Tony and I grab a bite to eat at the local wharf that was conveniently just outside the back door of the hotel. Tony was off for the evening to visit some friends in the area and I was alone for the first time in many weeks. Ironically being near the waters edge, I felt like a fish out of water. I grabbed a cup of coffee and the local newspaper and began to read the headlines. I read various stories from the political arena and about the war on terrorism. I felt sick after reading the paper and took a walk along the pier behind the hotel. I began to reflect on the journey I had just taken while thoughts of what I had just read in the newspaper began to bother me. I looked around as people leisurely strolled along the pier oblivious to the world outside their own. My thoughts reflected on my journey to Iraq and my blood began to boil.

From the moment I arrived in Iraq, my life seemed to change. To see our military's finest in action is something to see. To live the way they do and work in the environment they work in is something all together different from the recruiting commercials I had seen on television. On a daily basis, here in America, we take for granted what we have. We sleep in nice warm beds and use private bathrooms that have lots of running water for showers. We have our own private kitchens in which we store our own private stock of food, and in addition, let us not forget our air conditioners, to our respite from the heat of summer. Yet, in far-off distant lands, in other parts of the world, Americans are living in the desert with no access to the luxuries we have here at home. Do they complain about these conditions? Most definitely, they do; however, not in ways you would think. They long for the opportunity to taste that long forgotten beer or the home-cooked meal Mom makes for them, to feel running water flow over their bodies as they wash off the rough edges of the day, or to sit out on the porch and smoke that cigar as they listen to crickets chirping in the distance. Even though they long for home, their mission at hand is more important to them.

Many of the warriors we had the privilege to be with are second- and third-tour veterans of Iraq. "Why do they return?" you might ask. I asked that question many times throughout this journey. Each time I got similar responses: "There is still so much to do here for the people of Iraq." "You weren't here when the first vote took place. You did not feel the positive energy which took over this country with that one single act." "To see the short lines in the first vote become endless seas of citizens in line for the second vote." "To see the look upon their faces when they were handed toys, blankets, water and food; their appreciation showing in their warm smiles each and every time was heartwarming." "Just because there are fanatics out there trying to harm us, we are here for the people of Iraq, to help them achieve something greater." "These people have no electricity, no running water, and in most cases, not enough food to nourish themselves and their families. In these areas you can forget the luxury of air conditioners all together."

Their responses reminded me of a soldier I had interviewed over a year ago. He was about to leave for Iraq for his first tour of duty, and when asked what he was thinking about in preparing to go over there, his response was simple, "I can't do much with what I have, but so much can be done with what I do." This came from a twenty-year-old who had never been outside the United States of America. He was looking forward to helping to rebuild a nation and give its people a better way of life. Throughout my journey, I thought of Staff Sergeant David "Dago" Toruga. I wondered how many others like him touched the area I was in and if they too felt the same way. In their own way, they touched the lives of another human being and helped free a people from oppression.

I chuckled remembering the varied conversations I had with the Marines who are also history enthusiasts as I am. These young warriors relayed their own thoughts over this journey, expressing their desire to touch the lives of the Iraqi people. Many commented on how they might have felt on the creation of America during the American Revolutionary War, in how we as revolutionists strived and fought against oppression from the King. They mentioned many times how they felt as though they were like the founding fathers back then, fighting for what was right for people who could not fight for themselves. As this was coming from our future leaders, I was in awe. Never in my wildest dreams would I have ever thought of comparing the war on terrorism to that of our founding fathers' struggles; yet after hearing those warriors, I must agree with them to a point.

Their responses began to make me think even more as I sat on the pier. We are there for humanitarian reasons, something Americans take pride in, yet the American people still do not comprehend this aspect of the mission. To many Americans, we are only there for the destruction of another country in the name of terrorism. They do not realize that if we were not in Iraq, Afghanistan, or another country fighting terrorism where it breeds, we would be fighting in the streets of America. I wondered how they would feel if every time they left the safety of their homes and drove down the street only to stop at a stop sign, had to worry where the next IED was placed. How would they feel if such a device, that was created to destroy human beings, killed their children or loved ones? How would they feel if they knew when they went to their local mall, excited to buy that new, unnecessary trinket, that they really do not need, they could be killed by a suicide bomber, who on that day, decided it was his or her turn to kill hundreds of innocent people because someone told them to do it? How would they feel if they boarded a train, excited to go visit family, or take that long overdue vacation, only to find out that someone else had decided that day to place a bomb on a fast-moving vehicle – the very train they happened to be on – to shut down the train system and kill hundreds of people unnecessarily? Every

American should ask these questions each day as they take a breath of air into their lungs.

As I watched the seagulls foraging in the water in front of me, the sun began to go down, and for the first time in weeks, I began to feel cold and empty.

Soon after breakfast the next morning, we were off to the airport headed home. Tony and I said good-bye and I headed toward my gate. I was so busy writing notes that I never bothered to look around at any of the other travelers. I seemed to be in my own little world.

Usually when I travel, I try to get a seat on the aisle, but on this flight, I needed to sit near the window. It was morning when our flight took off from San Diego International Airport and the skies were clear across the country. I was so grateful to be back in the USA that I gazed out the window and watched the landscape as we headed east. I have traveled back and forth across this country dozens of times, but for the first time I truly noticed the landscape below. If you truly pay attention to the ground beneath you, the soil changes colors like leaves on a tree. I had never noticed this before. The hues shifted from golden yellow sands to various shades of brown over the mountain ranges of Utah and Colorado, to the beautiful canopy of greens and yellows of the flat farmlands of the heartland, while the rivers below glimmered as the sun reflected off their flowing waters, to the sprawling cities filled with people. The grass changed from a lime green to a darker green as the Blue Ridge Mountains came into view. Its peaks emphasized its vastness in blues and greens. As we began our decent into the Washington, DC area, my heart began to race, knowing a real bed was waiting for me at home.

I was finally home at last, and although I longed for the warmth of my own comfortable bed, I felt guilty for sleeping in it once I lay between the sheets. I woke up the next morning only to find myself sleeping on the floor. This routine would continue for about a week. Each night I would lie down in bed and never notice getting up during the night, only to find myself wrapped in the comforter on the floor the next morning.

CHAPTER 19
RULES OF ENGAGEMENT
CONTROVERSIAL TO MILITARY OBJECTIVES

"Combat," defined in the dictionary as "fight, contend, actively oppose, armed battle" has an entirely different definition in the current war – it is a softer-handed tactic, "return fire only if fired upon."

Throughout history, there have been individuals who have lead warriors into victory on the battlefield with honor and dignity; brilliant Generals with a "kick ass and take names" type of attitude. Generals who had a clear understanding of the complexities of war; especially what it is like to be a part of the ground forces on the front lines.

Ground forces, affectionately called, grunts or ground pounders, are the warriors who go out on patrol, putting their lives at risk before the enemy each day. Warriors are exposed to not only IED's, RPG's and small arms fire attacks, but also possible chemical exposure, all of which could kill or render them disabled. The weaponry and equipment might be different from previous wars, still the same "combat is combat" applies no matter how you look at it.

When orders come down from General Officers to seek out the enemy and if fired upon, attack with a fury, these warriors take pride in their ability and training to do their jobs with proficiency and accuracy. Unfortunately, times have begun to change because now, when a warrior follows such orders, they're subjected to being crucified for doing their jobs with such proficient accuracy.

Military personnel are becoming more concerned when entering into a combat zone asking themselves the "what if" question, "What if I should kill the wrong person – is it a combat casualty or murder?" This type of mindset begins to weigh heavy on their minds and they begin to doubt themselves and their training. This atmosphere breeds contempt, dishonor and most of all complacency among our troops. A possible murder charge in a combat zone is not what they signed up for, they joined to defend and protect, but the rules have now changed.

In previous wars, when military personnel received orders to kill the enemy it was plain and simple. Unfortunately, there seems to be a change in mission directives. On a weekly basis, the rules of engagement seem to be changing. One week it is kick ass and takes names, and the following week it is treat the enemy with respect and do not fire upon them unless you are fired upon first. Is this a real war or is it a computer game and we are just waiting to see who picks up the bar tab?

If we are going to send our troops into a combat zone, they should be allowed to do their job proficiently and effectively. We need to stop this soft-handed glove tactic and allow our forces to do what is necessary in a combat zone or not send them in at all.

When we allow an enemy to dictate how we conduct the Rules of Engagement, we have already lost the war. When we allow politicians to dictate these changes, we not only have lost the war, we have lost our credibility as a military power.

What the average American does not know is the enemy, insurgents and terrorists alike have our weapons in "their" hands. The insurgents have also studied our way of life; knowing what buttons to push to get a reaction from the American people. Therefore, when they kill, they kill with one thought in mind, compromise support of the American Forces while demoralizing those still in the field. They engage in uncontrolled violent or murderous behavior, and make it look as though our warriors have committed these crimes.

I do not know any service member who would tie the hands of an enemy behind their back and shoot them in the back of the head. That is "Execution style tactics." American Forces are not cowards; they do not use enforcer execution tactics. These are tactics of cold-blooded killers, who enjoy killing for a living, the terrorists.

What is going on in Iraq at this time is simple: on a daily basis, there are insurgents and terrorists infiltrating villages with one goal in mind; to instill fear in the hearts and minds of its inhabitants. If their message, to not work with coalition forces is not comprehended, they will select one family – father, mother and young children, and then slaughter them in order to make their message clearer. These same insurgents threaten to repeat this behavior, if the villagers do not accuse the infidels of these atrocities – the "infidels being American Warriors." These tactics not only destroy morale of those within the unit who are being falsely accused, but it also undermines the positive relationship between Armed Forces and the inhabitants of the village. This is the main objective of the insurgents; undermine the positive by instilling fear and negativity. Unfortunately, American politicians do not understand or recognize psychological warfare when it is slapping them upside the head.

The people of Iraq now see how insurgents and terrorists are using them as pawns, and the tides are beginning to turn against the insurgents. Iraqi citizens are continually turning in those who are known terrorists and insurgents throughout the country. For those who have been falsely accused, they have lost more than just morale; they have lost faith in the bond these warriors live by – The Brotherhood.

Rules Of Engagement (ROE)
As Set Forth by the Military

Level 1: Compliant (Cooperative). The subject responds and complies to verbal commands. Close combat techniques do not apply.

Level 2: Resistant (Passive). The subject resists verbal commands but complies immediately to any contact controls. Close combat techniques do not apply.

Level 3: Resistant (Active). The subject initially demonstrates physical resistance. Use compliance techniques to control the situation. Level three incorporates close combat techniques to physically force a subject to comply. Techniques include: Come-along holds, Soft-handed stunning blows, Pain compliance through the use of joint manipulation and the use of pressure points.

Level 4: Assault (Bodily Harm). The subject may physically attack, but does not use a weapon. Use defensive tactics to neutralize the threat. Defensive tactics include: Blocks, Strikes, Kicks, Enhanced pain compliance procedures, Impact weapon blocks and blows.

Level 5: Assault (Lethal Force). The subject usually has a weapon and will either kill or injure someone if he is not stopped immediately, and brought under control. The subject must be controlled by the use of deadly force with or without a firearm or weapon.

In the mindset of military personnel who are highly trained in hand-to-hand combat and the use of weapons, these new rules of engagement, are confusing. Why is it confusing you might ask? Because of "the 3 block warrior standards;" In the course of any given day, a warrior can be called upon to conduct humanitarian relief, be a law enforcement officer, or be engaged in an exchange of weapons fire all in the course of three city blocks. Therefore, split second decisions come into play and the ROE becomes more complex.

Although we have taken the adage of "win hearts and minds" in this war, there is something else that arises from these changes – possible Murder Charges?

In today's environment, when a warrior begins to second-guess his or her training, instead of concentrating on staying alert, alive and on guard and is more concerned about how the American people are going to react to their actions, it has the potential to be catastrophic.

I have said it many times over; the United States does not have enough body bags in the supply cabinet for the catastrophic aftermath of such soft-handed changes.

Throughout this war, there have been incidents, which were not called for and military justice prevailed, but there are many other cases, justice took a wrong turn in the end.

Those who are in charge of investigating these false allegations, have not only succumbed to egotistical behavior they have allowed themselves to become pawns for the enemy at hand. Why did they not bring forth the truth about the insurgent's involvement in certain murders? Instead, they went along with the political hierarchy and allowed this "form of set up" to prevail. When they let us down and convict the innocent warrior with premeditated murder, they have just allowed the enemy to win. The Game is over, we might as well pick up the bar tab and go home.

Many who read this book may not be familiar with the inner workings of psychological warfare. Allow me to put it into easier terms for better understanding, the main objective in Psychological Warfare is to Divided and Conquer. In the current war, the insurgents know Americans will cover their own individual ass first before they will cover another person's ass. The idea is to strip the vital essence of integrity, morality, and courage from each person one at a time, getting them to show their true colors as a person. These values are the very fabric of our military. You must have all three in order to be a cohesive unit. Therefore, they target them by manipulating and peeling away each of these values. What is their goal in doing this? It is to destroy the sacred trust between brothers; knowing one will lie and give false testimony to cover his or her own ass; or if given the opportunity to have revenge against another based on jealousy, achievement or personal character. In the end, they will have achieved their objective to destroy that silent code of trust.

Psychological warfare is further compounded when a service member is accused of murder in a combat zone, and then intimidated by our own investigating officials. The investigators become afraid that if they can't provide convictions, their own butts will be on the line, and their careers could be irreparably damaged. This snowballs when other members of the unit begin to testify. Although they are aware of the facts of the incident, some will cave to the pressure and intimidation by investigators and give false testimony. They are afraid if they don't comply, their own careers could be in jeopardy. Those who give false testimony, have to live with the knowledge they have turned their backs on a brother and live with the ramifications of their actions. Though they know there has been no murder committed, they have dishonored a brother by condemning him to life in prison.

Further humiliation and travesty falls upon our military when those in charge bring about wrongful charges of murder and misconduct. Look back in the news and you will find two such cases concerning the Marine Corps. The first dealt with an officer accused of the wrongful death of an Iraqi who was considered a hostile enemy before the shooting. Then you have the most horrific display of dishonor against the Marines stationed in Haditha. Seven Marines and one Corpsman charged with murdering individuals in a town – execution style.

Both these cases are prime examples of the enemy's psychological warfare tactics; subordinates who turned against brothers and gave false testimony in order to save their own ass in a military court. Plea bargains that saved them from hardship yet destroyed the trust within the ranks of their unit.

Although the ROE were right on target in the cases within the Army involving rape, unjustifiable murder and stupidity involving detainees, I have to pose the question as to these individuals maturity to even have been in the military in the first place. Have we lowered the standards of entry into the military because of the environment we are currently in, or has this country eroded morally that much?

If we continue to allow the psychological warfare machine of the enemy to predetermine how we run this war, we might as well give up the keys to the treasures of America and move out.

Historical Comparison: Too Close to Comfort?

During the Vietnam War, similar negligence, which showed no real leadership authority, or clear understanding of military operations, came out of the Pentagon. This caused serious distrust and as result, Congress got involved. We all know what happens when Congress gets involved with anything seriously important – they screw it up even more. All we have to do is look back into history and see the evidence. Throughout the sixties, many on Capitol Hill were former military who served during World War II and Korea and should have known, or understood the complexities of war. Instead, they were cowards and allowed their position and voices to become a destructive cause for further demoralization and continued accusations and distain towards our military forces.

In today's war, it is much the same as it was back during Vietnam. This time we have many more civilian workers without a clear understanding of our enemies to make rules and regulations to suit the needs of politicians and special interests. This form of reluctance to execute military responses will further hinder future retaliation from any attacks on our Armed Forces throughout the world and our own nation. We will ultimately lose credibility around the world and cease to be an effective military power.

For some reason politicians and civilian's alike believe that when a soldier, sailor, airman or Marine goes to war, they go with a romantic notion of obtaining a ribbon, or medal. I have no idea what military they are looking at, because I know of no service member who thinks like that. Unlike politicians, service members know that once the firefight begins, bullets that are fired from their weapon will ultimately be returned back in their direction. Combat is not like a political campaign; once the gloves come off, they must stay off until the fighting is complete.

There are some in the senior officer corps, who has an exaggerated sense of self-importance, who are more interested in political advancement rather than taking care of their warriors. These same officers have now secured their retirement and have gained civilian recognition on television as military analysts. Instead of speaking up about the problems while in uniform, they go before a camera, denounce our government and the mission at hand, all the while revealing military strategies, secrets, and put our Armed Forces in further danger. Out of all the former Generals I have seen on television since 2001, there has only been one who has refused to answer certain questions about tactical strategies and who did not give away the keys to the vault; General H. Norman Schwarzkopf.

Like my father used to say, "Any officer who is on active duty and is not willing to stand before any senior officer, or even the President of the United States, put his brass on the line and fight for his soldiers, doesn't deserve the rank of an officer on their shoulders!" He would continue on to say, "They are usually the corrupt, disorganized, self absorbed with no focus, no dedication to service, no discipline, no will, and surely no patriotism for ones country." Sounds like a politician in the making; does it not?

Please do not get me wrong there are many officers who have fought for their soldiers and who have suffered the consequences and repercussions of their actions. They are the officers you will never hear from on television, because they know that their words would help to kill American Service Members. There are the officers who understand that courage, devotion; bonds of love, misery, death and destruction are all born from combat.

War is War - Plain and simple! It is a brutal, dangerous existence, all the while testing skills, manhood, physical courage, and fortitude. It is to combat aggression, render humanitarian aid, and train troops. It is not romantic - it is dangerous.

When officers that are trained for combat are not allowed to implement that training, you have two results; a lost war and extensive amounts of casualties on the battlefield.

When civilians who have never been to war, trained for war or even thought of war are put in charge of a war, this will cause serious resentment among the troops, especially the officers. The reason for this is that the military is a very complex machine. Without the proper understanding of all phases and facets of how the military works, it is hard to give orders to those who know the intricacies and expect them to follow such orders without complaints.

Civilians who are clearly political appointees, or who work for the Department of Defense, some of whom are former military, fail to understand the complexities of combat life. Many of them have never been in a combat zone, nor do they care to understand the pitfalls of being in one. On a daily basis, these civilians continually tie the hands of those expected to lead service members into combat. As a result, our service members are prevented from performing their militarily trained objectives. When a civilian style no-win strategy clearly lacks any military understanding or capacity to do what needs to be done to safeguard the lives of service members, these political restraints render military leaders powerless.

Meanwhile others who make decisions do not know or understand the mindset and culture of the enemy at hand. These people do not want our Armed Forces to be victorious, because they are political in nature and not military minded. These same people leak information out to various media venues to further harm and ridicule those who put on the uniform every day. Should they not be called traitors?

Orders come down from Washington to the senior brass and on down through the ranks. The commanding officers are given a mission. Unfortunately, because Washington is involved, the orders aren't always given with a complete understanding of the whole situation. What is a service member or even senior brass to do when confronted with this disparity? Failure to stand up to unscrupulous or foolish orders could have "war crime" type repercussions, but service members are taught to take and hand down orders from the first boot camp day. From the top down, military personnel feel as thought they are dogs kept on a leash. Do as you are told, and only as you are told, don't think! When you keep a dog on a leash for too long, they can become complacent and may not perform very well when asked to do tricks.

One has to wonder about the philosophy and loyalties of these same civilians and senior brass. Is their primary focus to save enemy forces and placate politicians rather than safeguard American forces and move towards victory? This division of allegiance not only causes humiliation, it is extremely destructive to our military in the end.

CHAPTER 20
REVELATION BEGINS

April 2006

On a daily basis, we meet people, many we connect with, others we do not. Many times, we dismiss a person because he, or she, does not fit into our life for political reasons. This is a shame, because unless we are willing to take the journey to explore the real reasons why we met a person, we could miss the possibility of them being a very important part of our lives, personally or professionally. Have you ever had a chance meeting with someone who you knew, deep in your soul, was someone very special? Not realizing at the time what an important role, that person would play in your life, maybe they even help to change your life, or achieve a goal of a lifetime.

It was not until I returned home that I realized just how lucky I had been recently. I began to take stock in those around me. This meant a lot of soul searching. Meanwhile, many friends and colleagues began to ask questions about the trip; what it was like politically, socially, economically and militarily. One question, which was consistent, was if I was scared, or afraid. The answer was always the same surprisingly - I was not.

Why wasn't I afraid, I wondered? At first, I thought it was because I mentally prepared myself for what to expect. Then I thought well, maybe it was because the Marines who surrounded me were highly qualified to take care of any situation. Maybe it was because I travel so much, never worrying about anything, but just enjoying the trip. That might have had a lot to do with it, but deep down I knew it was something else. The more I tried to figure it out, the more I smiled.

I was blessed years ago when one person came into my life, during one of those chance meetings. During the initial introduction, there was a feeling of instantaneous trust and I felt safer than I had ever felt with anyone. This was rare for me. Over the years, our friendship got stronger and stronger. Although I knew of his accomplishments in the military, they were never the foundation of our friendship. It was the trust I felt secure with and I knew I could say anything to this man and it would stay between us. That trust between us bonded our friendship.

Over the years, I never thought of him as playing such a key role in my life until I was invited to join the Marines in Iraq. Therefore, it was obvious why I was not afraid, or scared on my trip; for the first time in my life I brought someone with me –a friend. Someone I trusted enough that I didn't hesitate placing my life and all I hold dear in his hands for the entire trip. In a combat zone, if you cannot trust those around you to watch your back, you are dead. Knowing that he had my back at all times, gave me a tremendous amount of relief that allowed me to be creative and concentrate on my work. Just knowing he was never far, gave me strength and courage to accomplish my goals, as we traveled around a combat zone. His confidence encouraged me to take risks I never would have taken if I were alone. This was a first for me.

I realize as I write these words, that if the timing was off by one day, I probably would have been scared to take this journey alone. Instead, the stars lined up perfectly and he was able to join me. I am forever grateful for not only our friendship, but also the trust our friendship has given us over the years. I would never have achieved my goal, or felt as safe as I did, if Tony had not been there for me on this journey.

One thing everyone should experience is taking a once in a lifetime journey with someone you can trust. When I travel alone I never have the opportunity to share the wonderful experiences afforded me, which is why I was blessed to have shared this experience with Tony. I now understand what our military means when they say it is a brotherhood of trust because of the bond we have with each other. It is a very powerful feeling to have for another person.

Before I left on this journey, a dear friend, who is a Vietnam Veteran, said this experience would change my life forever. At the time, I had laughed, thinking it never would, but he was so right. Many of the soldiers who I have dealt with said similar things. One comment stood out from all of them, "Maybe when you come back you will then understand the world I am living in right now." He was right; I did not understand this until I returned home.

In dealing with our returning soldiers over the years, I could not put myself in their shoes because I had never been to combat. Although I tried to understand why they changed so drastically, I could never relate, nor comprehend the changes a person has upon coming home. Now I think I understand with a bit more clarity what they have been trying to say.

Let me try to put into words how I was feeling, thinking and reacting upon coming home. My experience is by far so much less than anyone who has ever put on a uniform and gone to war, but many I have spoken to since returning, who have been in uniform, have made the same comment "Welcome to my world!" Never in my wildest dreams could I have imagined this experience would truly change my life so much, but it did.

I found myself looking at every aspect of my life differently. In Iraq, I saw birds and wondered why I never heard them singing. At home, for the first time I began listening to the birds as they sang and watched them fly from tree to tree outside my office window. I found myself enjoying the beauty of the foliage as it springs to life after being dormant from winter. I noticed I was not on the internet as much and enjoyed the beauty that surrounded me.

I have always been a people watcher wherever I went, be it a bar, airport or the mall. For some reason, I am now seeing people differently for the first time. The week of my return, I joined a few friends for our weekly happy hour gathering at a local sports pub. I was not the happy-go-lucky life-of-the party this time. Instead, I was much quieter then usual; I was observing how people were interacting with each other. I noticed when they smiled falsely as they listened to trivial stories of work, life, and whatever else was being said to them. I observed people's table manners and etiquette I had never taken note of before. It was not the clothing I noticed, but the way they tried to appear to be something they were not. I found myself not only looking at them, but also the traffic on the street, becoming more and more conscious of the vehicles parked along the curb. The noises began to bother me, and I felt my chest beginning to cave in. I was in a place I did not want to be. This is when I realized I was not ready to be around people just yet. I wanted to be alone for a while.

A few nights later, I decided to join some friends at an Irish pub for dinner. The pub was crowded as usual. Normally I would have relished walking through the crowd meeting and greeting new people along the way, while I waited for my friends. Instead, I stood alone by the door. Another friend walked in and invited me to join him and his friends from the State Dept instead of standing by the door. Joining them turned out to be a mistake. They all had questions about the journey and my experiences. While I shared tales of the trip, one man who worked for the State Dept had to make 'his knowledge' known to all and explained my assessment of the situation in Iraq was not accurate. Having never been there, he apparently knew it all. His position in the government was of no real significance when it came to national security issues pertaining to terrorism, or even the region where I had been.

However, he began spouting off about how bad it was in Iraq. He began challenging me 'about the fact' an insurgent, just that morning had blown up a Mosque in Baghdad and killed over a hundred people. As he spoke, I began to laugh. His rendition of the facts, as he knew them, was very inaccurate. This is the most serious problem in this country. Repeating what we hear on the news without checking the facts. He was repeating the news that was reported that morning.

As I began to laugh, my friend gave me a funny look. Before he or anyone else could ask why I was laughing, I gave them the answer. This highly intelligent man, who works for a federal agency, sipping his beer in-between his words, was way off base. I explained that I was on the phone with the Public Affairs Office (PAO) in Baghdad that morning when the story broke by the reporter who was in Baghdad. I inquired about the facts and asked what the true story was. Not only was my PAO contact in Iraq upset, he was livid at the reporter for reporting it the way he did. The PAO cut the conversation with me short to go take care of the reporter. When he called me back, I heard the real story. The true story was; "Yes, there was an insurgent who strapped a bomb to his person and walked into a building that killed people. The building was located four buildings away from the Mosque, but only one person was killed besides himself." That's some reporting, huh? The reporter was sent home that morning, and was placed on the barred list for reporting a false story.

One would think if someone worked for the federal government, he or she would be educated or equipped to analyze information better. Here lies the problem with our country; we only hear what we want to hear. Instead, he had memorized the crap word for word. Talk about easily led down a path, which truly has us, ignorant on facts because we always seem to believe everything on the news or in the papers.

Later that same night as I drove home, my thoughts were again drifting to the Marines overseas. As I approached a traffic light in the dead of night, near the Pentagon, there was a quick burst of light, which lit up the sky. At first I was freaked out, and then it happened again. It was only lightening, but for a brief moment, because my thoughts were back in Iraq, I was not sure where I was. This reaction was not what I expected. I later received a call from one of the soldiers I had been speaking to for over a year when he found it difficult to sleep. I told him what happened and to my surprise, he laughed at me. Although we did not see heavy fighting, geez, I slept through a mortar attack; he told me that was a normal reaction. I relayed to him that I find myself still scanning the streets as I drive down the road, again he laughed at me, and said he still does the same thing. Then he made the most telling comment, "welcome to our world, Betty." I told him I was not sure whether I was actually in his world or not. I felt sheltered, but grateful at the same time. We were in a place that had been secured by the Warriors who had been stationed there. He reminded me it was the adrenaline rushing through my veins and it would take time to subside from the high I had been on for the last month. Then it dawned on me, he was right. Without realizing it, the adrenaline was flowing and I did not recognize it. I should have known better.

Anyone who knows me, knows that I am usually very outgoing and flirtatious, always harassing the men around me to put a smile on their face. I'm a practical joker too, playing tricks on my friends in order to make them laugh, or take the edge off a bad situation.

While sharing my recent experiences with the wife of a soldier still serving in Iraq with the 4th Alabama and how I survived being surrounded by so many good looking Marines, I forwarded her a picture of me surrounded by some of them. As she opened the email and looked at the picture, I continued to explain the conditions in which we lived. Her response after looking at the picture cracked me up. She called me "A female Hugh Heffner." I had to laugh at the reference. I remarked that Hugh Hefner lounges in silk, surrounded by scantly dressed beautiful females and could not see the correlation. Yes, good-looking Marines surrounded me all the time, but I was sweating in layers of body armor and Desert Camo's, with no make up, no nails and let's not forget the sensual perfume of O'de sweat, hardly living the life of Hugh Heffner. But, it was good to laugh.

Iraq was more than a revelation about our military; it was also a revelation into who I am as a person. I learned many lessons from the Marines I was with one thing was to always tell those who have touched your heart how much they mean to you. I had many in my life who have touched my heart and a few of them lived in Massachusetts. What better time is there to deliver such a message, than over the Easter Weekend? I took the first flight out as fast as I could.

There is something very special to me about Massachusetts. As I cross the state line, an overwhelming feeling takes hold of my heart; it's a feeling of coming home. Here is where I find the most peace in life. The people of Massachusetts are the warmest, most loving and friendly people I have ever met. I am lucky to have many friends in this area to make my visits that much more special. Whenever I feel the need for grounding, this is where I escape. There is no place I know where the sounds of the ocean crashing against the rocks and the ocean breeze, crisp and fresh, can put peace and harmony back into your veins better than Plymouth Massachusetts. Here you can not only regain a better perspective on life and become centered, but if you like, chowder and seafood this area has the best in all of New England.

The weather in Plymouth, Massachusetts was beautiful that weekend. The ocean was crisp and luscious as usual, enticing me to stand in its waters edge and allow it to wash away the overwhelming burdens I had felt since returning from Iraq. That is exactly what I did. As the cold water rushed over my bare feet, the oceans breeze softly kissed my check. I finally felt as though I was truly home.

My dear friends, Linda and Paul McAlduff welcomed me home with open arms. Linda commented almost immediately that something was different about me; I was not as hurried as I had been on previous visits. I was taking things slower and noticing things more. As we visited, Linda mentioned a street corner dedication scheduled for the next day. It was for a mutual friend's son, who was killed in Iraq a few years earlier. Since I just returned from the same area in which he was killed, I felt the urge to attend. Not many in the area knew I was back and I could surprise them by showing up.

The next morning I arrived at the site of the dedication and wasn't immediately recognized me with the short hair. I noticed this but it did not bother me at all since I was not interested in interacting with anyone just yet. While many wondered who the woman was standing alone, a few did a double take recognized me. While the speakers spoke, Tony appeared behind me to say hello and asked if I had been up in a CH53 lately or not. I chuckled at the reference and knew he could not hold back from picking on me about that one embarrassing moment in my life. This dedication was like many other dedications I had attended.

But, there was one important difference, I could now relate to the Marine it was in honor of, because he had given the ultimate sacrifice in Fallujah, in the same Province I had spent the last month.

Later that evening, while I drove back to Linda and Paul's home, I stopped the car in the middle of the private road on which they lived. For the first time, I noticed the moon flickering over the water in the bay. I noticed how the tall grass in the marsh swayed in such a way that it reminded me of one of Mozart's piano concertos. I realized I was taking time for me for the first time in my life. The next morning I noticed the vibrant colors of the flowers in the garden and the way the birds were flittering over the birdbath outside the window. When I went back into town that morning, I took one last stroll around Plymouth Bay, watching the boats in the choppy waters. The tourists were seeking out keepsakes in the shops nestled along the road. I began reflecting upon the beginnings of our great nation as I looked down upon the Plymouth Rock. How much the country has changed since those first explorers stepped off the boat onto a new land.

CHAPTER 21
DEPRESSED SOCIETY

It was heartbreaking to leave, but commercial airlines do not wait for any passenger and I headed to the airport. When I traveled in the past, like many others, I could be seen in the airport terminal, a cell phone hanging from my ear, pecking away at the keys of my laptop not paying attention to anyone around me. This time was different; I sat and watched people scurrying around the gate area. To my astonishment, I saw something for the first time, everyone was in a hurry, but there was no place to go. Each had an attitude as they fiddled with cell phones, PDA's and their laptops hanging off various parts of their bodies. I cringed, because that used to be me. I watched people's body language, listened to the tone of their voices as they interacted with people. There was a feeling in the air that struck me to the core.

A woman on the phone discussed her relationship with a friend on the other end. It seemed to be a romantic relationship, from what I gathered. She complained about how her boyfriend would not pay attention to her; treats her like crap, and walks all over her, yet he had the nerve to ask for favors all the time. Her friend must have asked her a question because her reply was – "I do them to please him, yet he never thanks me, or shows his appreciation for what I have done for him." She quietly began to cry into the phone, telling her friend that she just does not understand how much she loves this man and what she was doing wrong that he not love her in return. I just sat there shaking my head when the word "disrespect" came to mind.

Another complained about her family – From what I could gather, her older sister gave her problems over the holiday when she announced she wanted to move to somewhere in the mid west. "The schools are better, taxes are extremely lower and as a single mother, I could give my kids a better life." She said. Her Sister and Mother were appalled with the idea – complaining how "they" would never see her or the kids. She sounded confused and not so sure of her self any more. What should she do, she asked her friend. She was so sad about a decision she seemed to want to make—I felt for her and the word "selfishness" came to mind.

Then there was a young mother sitting on the floor playing with her young daughter; singing to her to keep her occupied until we boarded. This was the only person in the terminal who smiled.

Two annoying men were so busy with conversations on their cell phones; they became impatient, waiting to board the Southwest Flight. They repeatedly asked why the line was not moving. They failed to realize that the plane had not landed yet. The word "self-important" came to mind.

For some reason, I yearned to be back in Iraq, where at least the people were more pleasing, polite and much nicer.

After boarding the plane, I waited for my fellow passengers to take their seats. I then began to sympathize with those who worked for the airlines, wondering to myself how baggage handlers were able to hold onto their jobs since no one checked baggage anymore. Then I thought, hell every college student should go after those jobs, they can work their scheduled hours and still study, 'cause they apparently do not have much to do since everyone brings their suitcases, large and small with them into the cabin of the plane. That is when I realized how selfish my fellow passengers were. His or her time was more important than anyone else's was on the plane. Then it hit me like a brick, these were the same people who were complaining how long it taken the others to get off the plane. Selfish individuals who were bringing full suitcases on board and making the rest of us wait, while they struggled to lift and push a suitcase into the overhead compartment. Compartments that were not made to fit full size suitcases. I wanted to scream and recommend that they help the economy and save a baggage handler's job. I know one thing; my suitcase had first class treatment, being the only one in the luggage compartment without any of those other nasty bags around it.

One observation was consistent; no one smiled. Every passenger looked depressed and sad. The atmosphere within the airport and the plane was that of a sad society.

When I arrived back in DC, I could feel not only the heat of the day, but something more stifling. The atmosphere in this city is unlike any other city. Washington, DC is a city filled with so much negativity it can suffocate a person. One would think it is the hot air emanating from the buildings. In reality, it is the negativity radiating from politicians. The negativity and their complacency shows on the faces of everyone in this city. If only they would look into the eyes of the people who elected them, politicians might see the sadness, which shows in their eyes, it is earth shattering.

CHAPTER 22
LIFE MOVES IN A NEW DIRECTION

When a person returns from a combat zone, no matter what they were there for, life changes for them in many ways. They view every aspect of their life differently. They begin questioning their careers and the direction they are going. Questions concerning their love life come full circle. They wonder if the person they are involved with is the right person for them. Many admit to their feelings having changed while they were away, or to some their feelings have gotten even stronger. I mentioned that my life changed just like many others. My outlook on life and opinion on many issues are quite different now. While my professional life is prospering, my personal life has changed dramatically.

Many Soldiers I have spoken with over the last few years have discussed the many signs put before them, signs they overlooked in the past. While life is falling back into place for so many, these signs appear before them in a very special way, maybe to help ease the burden of transition. These very special signs have always been there in order to help define who we are as a person, so we can find the answers to life's many questions. While other times we are given a very special gift by a messenger from our past. One of those gifts I received upon my return home.

An old friend called and invited me to join him for dinner, to share the tales of my exciting journey and to catch up on life in general. I accepted his invitation gladly because it had been a number of years since we had seen each other, and because he had been in Iraq in recent years too.

Over dinner, we compared notes of our shared experiences in Iraq and talked about the political issues surrounding the war.

Since I was out of the country, he caught me up on the happenings of the inner circle of DC. The subject then turned to our personal lives and I shared a few things I had not noticed before my trip. He sat across from me, sipping his Merlot, explaining how he had been going through a revelation of his own lately and began to pour out his heart. After returning home from Iraq, he went through a divorce, and began cleaning out the closets of his life. During this cleansing process, he realized many things about himself and that he had fallen in love with someone from his past, but did not know what to do about it.

Part of his healing meant cleaning out the closets of his life, even the real ones in his home. A powerful revelation came to him when he found a box buried deep in the back of his closet, containing his special keepsakes he long treasured. A few hours went by before he looked inside and found letters from someone he once knew. He reread them repeatedly, only to realize in a very powerful way what was missing in his life; he had failed to communicate what was in his heart.

Through each letter he read from a woman in his past, he learned that sharing what is in ones heart can be very special to another person, especially the one you care about. During their courtship, she traveled extensively, and she wrote to him, sharing what was happening in her life. At the time he was not interested in what was happening in her life, only his own. He admitted that while rereading those letters, he began to understand what an ass he had been and how much he had screwed up a wonderful relationship. He also admitted that the one thing she craved in their relationship, he never gave to her. He thought he did everything right, doing what every perfect man should do, buying her things and taking her places. When all the while he was missing the boat on what she really wanted from him, an intimate relationship.

When he was finished, he realized he had fallen in love with the woman who had opened her heart and shared her soul with him. She took the time to share herself and for that, he was grateful. That was not all that he realized from her letters. He remembered during that time, she traveled a lot and their quality time together was limited. He was in a needy stage in his life, selfish about everything. He needed to be with a person in his life all the time, for both political and social reasons, but she was not available to be there for him in body, only in spirit. He resented her for this and ultimately began seeing someone else. Yet, after reading her letters, he realized she had known this and in her way, she was with him all the time, through her written words. By sharing her life and her heart with him, she showed how much she cared. She shared her heart in a very special way. He could see her sitting in that airport, or hotel, describing her adventures and experiences, even how she was feeling at the time.

Although at the time of their relationship, he was frustrated with his career and all he wanted to do was scream or yell. Instead of yelling back, she wrote him letters because she did not solve problems by yelling. Back then, he did not see it, but now he did. The woman he chose as a life partner was not his partner in any sense of the word. For security concerns, he was not capable of sharing his life with her, personal or professional, and unfortunately, the marriage fell apart.

Upon returning home that evening, I checked my voice mail for messages. To my surprise, there were a few messages from my friend whom I just had left. The first was to thank me for listening and said he was going to call the woman shortly to see if she was possibly available to rekindle a new relationship with him. I smiled. However, the second message from him knocked me off my feet completely. He had called her all right. The message he left was: "The lady in question you know intimately, it is you." I could not believe my ears. The third message was that special gift I mentioned, "I know you have moved on with your life and I am very happy for your successes. I wanted you to know that the light bulb finally went off. Now I know what I lost and what you were trying to tell me all those years ago. Thank you! Your friendship is valued so much more now, and I truly want it to be a part of my life, now and forever." I sat on my sofa staring at the phone, not believing my ears.

I could not help but smile at his messages. Life is all about timing after all. People come into your life for a reason. You never know what rewards you are to reap from knowing them. We never know what part they will play, even though silently we fall in love with them, but never say the words. I was happy that something I wrote so many years ago helped him heal in the final stages of his personal transformation. As he said in a subsequent conversation, it helped him become a man who can truly open his heart and share what is inside his heart.

If his realization had happened before I left for Iraq, I probably never would have gone on this trip and spent the rest of my life with this man. He was right though; I had changed and moved on. I was not the same woman he once knew. His goals and aspirations were completely different from mine. If I had been the same woman he once knew, I probably would have picked up the phone and rekindled that lost romance with the man who just admitted to being in love with me. Why not? He is gorgeous, wealthy and extremely accomplished. He would have given me the world if I asked for it. However, life changed dramatically during my trip to Iraq and I am no longer the same woman he once knew. Our goals and aspirations were no longer the same.

CHAPTER 23
QUESTIONS BEGIN

Friends and colleagues asked many questions about my thoughts on the reconstruction of Iraq. Repeatedly, I was asked, "if we should be there or not" and, "how the conditions over there could be compared to the way of life here in America." So many times, I wanted to give them a history lesson, instead I gave them the politically incorrect response.

"As much as I want to compare, I think you should be more interested in looking at the flaws of our own country, before you judge a country which is going through growing pains." They never liked that response. They did not like this response either, "Before we can look at another country and find fault, we must be willing to open our eyes and admit to our own flaws, which are buried deep within our own roots." In order for one to understand, they must look back into history, at the founding fathers struggles, and ask how those struggles were endured to get us to where we are today.

One night while trying to struggle with the many questions people were throwing at me, I began to clean out my old files and resurrected something I wrote many years ago. While keeping the original theme, I updated it with current issues and decided to include it in this book. When I originally wrote it, I never realized how important it would become to how I felt after I came home from this journey.

The United States of America is a nation created by people with old world style and values. Some were adventurous, craving a new challenge, while others wanted a new way of life. It is a fabulous story to be told over, and over again, but for some reason we are not teaching this in our schools. Why do we allow ourselves to forget the sacrifices that were made for us over the years? The blood that was shed to sustain the liberties and the freedoms we now take for granted each day!

As I travel this great country, I can still see the vast bounty that inspired the settlers to strive and ultimately survive so long ago. Strive for a better life than what they left behind. You can rediscover the majestic views that were once discovered by Lewis and Clark. Yet, we never seem to stop and enjoy them as often as we should. We find ourselves exploring other lands without understanding our own backyards. As our children learn about our history in school, we leave it up to teachers to teach them about this great nation, some of whom have never taken the time to see the beauty it has to offer first hand. They teach from books instead of life experience.

Take the Washington, DC area for example: I am fortunate to live in an area of Virginia that affords me the pleasure of visiting and revisiting so many historical sites in this area. With so much history surrounding us, one can always find something new to explore everyday. I can walk the streets of Alexandria where George Washington, Thomas Jefferson, John Adams, and the Marquis de Lafayette once walked. The old structures and cobble-stoned streets give your imagination the opportunity to wonder, "What part of history happened within that brick and mortar?"

As I walk through the streets of the most powerful city in the world, Washington DC, I cannot help but feel the power of James Madison, John Adams, Thomas Jefferson and Abraham Lincoln, who once walked these same streets! It is overpowering at times to think, that from the hopes and visions of this new land of promise, these men shaped the great country we now call home.

I often find myself returning to two very special sites nearby, to help give me the peace and tranquility I need to survive in this town; these are the United States Marine Corps Memorial and Arlington National Cemetery. They remind me of the sacrifices that have been made so I can be free. It never fails to amaze me as I gaze out over the majestic view of the Potomac River to see our nation's capitol, the beauty and spender of the monument's lights flickering under the moonlight. *"History transcends time when one looks out over this magnificent city,"* Charles Dickens once said. He once described this city to a friend in a letter dated 1842, *"It is sometimes called the City of Magnificent Distances, but it might with greater propriety be termed the City of Magnificent Intentions."*

This is the most powerful city in the world, but to me it's home. It is powerful, eclectic and diverse all at the same time! When both House and Senate are in session, there are people from all over the country and all occupations scurrying around the city. There are young staffers, who come with amazing hopes and dreams of making a difference. Lobbyists, who represent special interests groups, focus on wanting to gain more power and greed. Politicians, like their staffers, come in wearing rose-colored glasses, only to realize they cannot accomplish what they set out to do in one term. It seems nothing ever gets accomplished from one election to another, except an never-ending circle of compromise and favor-trading because they gradually sell their souls to continue getting back into office, until they can't do the good they set out to do, and still keep the promises elicited to get them back into office.

Although the view evokes an overwhelming sense of pride in one's heart, it is a double edge sword; both comforting, yet scary at the same time. I often wonder what our founding fathers would say if they could sit with me and review what has become of their precious new world. Would they be able to tell me where we went wrong in the last sixty years? Were we have allowed ourselves to chip away and destroy the very foundation they left us?

Historians will say the early 1700's was a rough existence, for some reason, I cannot believe this. It was a gratifying and simpler lifestyle. They had the ability to create everything they needed to survive; from their clothes and furnishing, to the candles that allowed them to read at night. Although they struggled to endure, they were grateful to be in a new land they could call their own. They had every right to be grateful, they worked for everything and it was theirs, a making of their own two hands. As a community they worked together to grow crops and raise their animals. Granted they did not have the luxuries that we have today. Could we live without air conditioning on those hot summer days? What about living without running water, electricity that runs everything; heat, televisions, cordless telephones, hair dryers or even alarm clocks? Could we live without our current transportations systems? Let's not forgot the convenience of the grocery store where everything we consume has been grown, picked, bottled and shipped right to us. Do not overlook the internet, where everything we do is wrapped around e-mails and storage of personal files for faster and more convenient ways of communication. Oh and one cannot disregard our precious cellular phones. Could we survive without these luxuries as they did? I doubt it! The majority of our generation would be devastated.

Although the luxuries we enjoy today were inspired by small inventions, most of which were created by some of our founding fathers, and the brilliant people who came after them. Somehow, along the way, we seem to have forgotten the reasons why. Instead of reflecting, we tend to concentrate on materialistic items, rather than the purpose and reasons why this country was created in the first place.

Thanks to men like Jefferson, Franklin, Adams, Pierce, and Washington, who were rebels in their day, they fought for freedom from political and religious persecution and eventually won. Although they labored over the potential ramifications of their actions, they also discussed various social and economic issues, before deciding on how this country should be governed. As they debated over long-range issues, their main concern was for independence, versus immediate results and their next election. Some of our current day politicians should take a lesson from these men in looking at the good of the nation versus their own personal agenda.

One has to wonder what would have happened back then if they had the luxuries of today. Would they have been able to accomplish what they set out to do in less time? Maybe they could. It took ten years, but they created a country with a solid foundation to govern by, and that same foundation has sustained us until now.

Comparison:

I found myself rereading the Declaration of Independence and the Constitution these men created on our behalf. Although I read these documents in grade school, I forgot just how brilliant these men were. It was evident that the Religious freedoms we enjoy today were very important to these men back then. Their religious beliefs gave them the ability to understand that a higher being was the "Creator," which is why they highlighted this word and the following statement in this famous document, *"Laws of Nature and of Nature's God entitle them a decent respect to the opinions of Mankind."* This was and still is the foundation of this great nation. By including this statement in the Declaration of Independence, these men created this country to be protected by a being higher than one self; not a King, nor President, no man or woman that lives on this earth! This statement also gave us the "unalienable right" to worship any God we choose to worship, the God that lives in our hearts, while instilling the freedoms and values that would eventually create a stronger unity of our very own. In those times, although they were rebels by today's standards, these men were true visionaries! They created this country to be better than the oppressor they fought to get rid of. Yet, we as Americans have allowed our present day elected officials to chip away at the foundation they created. Now I wonder what will be left for our children and generations to come.

It is very interesting to compare then and now, only to see all the obstacles they had before them, and were able to accomplish the creation of a new government. With today's bureaucratic obstacles, it is a wonder our representatives in Washington get anything accomplished. They are not visionaries as those men once were, they cannot accomplish one percent of these men's accomplishments in their whole lifetime.

If we were to compare our past to the present, we would realize that we were given the rights and protections from a world of oppression and religious persecution. This shield also protected us from a monarchy or dictator with rules and regulations that would have held us back for many years to come. Somewhere along the way, we lost sight of the reasons why this country came to be. By doing this, we have taken for granted what they selflessly sacrificed to give us. Precious freedoms they struggled to leave us, as Americans, we have somehow overlooked and taken for granted because we were born here. This is a strong heritage we have been born into, but so many refuse to understand and appreciate. Power and greed has taken hold of this country and for the right dollar amount, we are willing to sell off our land and freedoms to the highest bidder, even if the buyer isn't a citizen of this country.

Each Forth of July marks the day in which we, as Americans, celebrate our independence from the old world and our independent governance over this new land. It is a day in which we are to remind ourselves that a group of men took it upon themselves to stand up for what they believed was right and declared our independence. Today, it seems to have taken on a different meaning: a day off from work to watch colorful fireworks, enjoy that annual cook out with our family and friends, and to some, dusting off that American Flag.

Over the years, I have seen a decline in parents teaching their kids about the heritage of this great nation. Parents do not talk about the sacrifices that were made for us to celebrate this day. Nor do they discuss the blood that was shed, or even the reasons why it was shed. A few years ago, while discussing this problem with a friend, his lady friend stood along side us and confessed that she was embarrassed with her nine year old son's response when he was asked, "Do you know what the Forth of July means?" his reply, "I get presents?" Although she was embarrassed to give his answer, she knew she had a lot of work to do to instill a sense of pride in her son's heart! Until that moment, she thought the schools were teaching this kind of stuff. I could not believe my ears! Here was an American Citizen, intelligent and well educated, who was under the impression that it was the responsibility of our school system to teach her son a sense of pride in his own country. She was a few years older than I was and I could not believe my ears! How can any American born citizen believe the school system should be responsible to hand down one's legacy! The school system is only partly to blame in failing to teach our children a sense of pride through American History education. Our educational system allows teachers to interject their political views rather than insisting they take pride in their country and teaching civic pride! Therefore, it is the responsibility of each parent to teach their children about civic pride, it is the responsibility of every parent to pass this pride onto their children!

Each of us in our own way can relate to so many things our founding fathers enjoyed. Passion for gardening as Jefferson and Washington; a love of reading as Jefferson, John Adams, Franklin and Payne; disgust for injustices as Samuel Adams despised and of course a love of writing as they all enjoyed. Unfortunately, we do not give enough of these men credit for their accomplishments. Many writers try to destroy their credibility, because they were our first politicians. Therefore, they tend to want to find the dirt and destroy their true accomplishments, instead of realizing that they had their faults as all men and women do. We all know from our own recent history, each politician begins their career with love of country in their hearts and want to make a difference, while being the voice of the people. It is not until they come to the magnificent city that they realize the true reality and impossibility of accomplishing what they set out to do.

Today - Power Versus Greed

We, as a nation, have become wrapped up in our daily lives, trying to survive. We have forgotten to look at the bigger picture of what is happening around us. Today's motto is "if it does not concern us at this moment, why bother getting involved?" Therefore, we can only blame ourselves as we allow our basic liberties and freedoms to be destroyed. Social issues that have been neglected since World War II have continued to be overlooked and are chipping away at the very essence of our country's foundation. A thirst for power and greed plagues us as Americans and allows our historical pride to be destroyed, while essential liberties are taken away from us with every breath we take. How could we have allowed these issues to take a toll on our country with little chance of regaining what has been lost?

Issues We Need to Address Here at Home.

We have allowed the First Amendment of the Constitution – "Freedom of Speech" to be misused and abused. Responsibility of one's actions is no longer the subject of respect. Speaking out against the government when a travesty has come to light is one thing, but to allow frivolous acts of disrespect that result in lawsuits claiming First Amendment Right violations are ludicrous. On a daily basis, we continue to allow cases to be brought before our courts based on freedom of speech infringements that include; disrespecting private property, defacing national monuments, all because they wanted their personal fifteen minutes of fame before the cameras. It seems if an argument sounds good and is good enough for a lawyer to get their name into the law books, they will bring a case forward, so they can set precedents for future cases. Judges, who wish to clear their dockets or gain recognition, misuse their power as a Justice to create laws or precedents rather than uphold or interpret the existing body of law; sometimes even granting an award for a stupid claim in the bargain. One has to wonder if our legal system has completely lost its perspective on what its role is in the three branches of government, over-reaching far into legislative or law making rather then being judges.

When the Founding fathers included the Second Amendment for us to Bare Arms, it was not their intent for each American to bare an Uzi, or a machine gun. This Amendment was to bare arms against invading forces in the protection of their families, property and freedoms. Many Americans hate the National Rifle Association for their lobbying to keep the Second Amendment alive. This is because most do not understand this amendment! I happen to agree 100% with the Second Amendment! We must uphold our rights as Americans to bare arms against an invading force, more so today than ever before. This amendment was not created to aid the objective of every drug dealer and criminal in the country. Making guns illegal prevents honest citizens from baring arms, criminals will break the law to get what ever they want, that's what makes them criminals. This is a social issue needs to be addressed separately from the second amendment. If we eliminate it together as a nation, maybe politicians will stop using the criminal element as a smoke and mirror issue to cover up their faults on Capitol Hill.

During the Great Depression, President Roosevelt created what was called, "The New Deal Act." The New Deal Act was to help those less fortunate provide a living for themselves as well as their family. I cannot believe his original intent was for people to be on this program for twenty or thirty years. Nor do I think he intended to have the government take advantage of American citizens by violating their 4th and 14th Amendment rights. A portion of this New Deal turned into the Welfare program, which was later renamed Social Services.

Social Services and Welfare is a problem all its own. There are many cases of power and greed running rampid throughout a system of financial incentives and lack of accountability. An investigation into social workers' gross misconduct and neglect should be conducted, before another child is put in danger by this system. Although there are many cases of actual abuse, something I do not condone in any way, there are thousands upon thousands of unsubstantiated cases brought against innocent people. Some of these unsubstantiated cases are cases brought against our military personnel who have been accused of abandonment because they are serving their country in either Iraq or Afghanistan.

How do we Change Things?

As a Nation, we must be willing to step up to the plate and personally take responsibility in the initiative to preserve our history and guard against the loss of our liberties. We can no longer expect our elected officials to watch out for us and protect the unalienable rights we are so worried about losing. We as a community must begin to question major issues that affect us all and ask ourselves how they relate to our neighbors as individual Americans before making a final decision. One

- 169 -

cannot expect our government to do everything for us, because if we leave it up to them, our voices will never be heard. This in and of itself is a dilution of rights. It is time to begin to look at the future and let your voices be heard. Until we address these issues separately, with calm voices, they will not go away. The one right every American has is their right to vote. Do not allow that right to be taken away too. Do not vote for a political party, vote for the individual who you feel in your heart will represent you and your rights as a citizen of the United States of America. We need representatives to represent us all, not their own personal agenda. Representatives who will stand up and go through the security check points the same, as you and I do, without incident or making it an issue of race or religion. Representatives, who will take action to preserve our rights and benefits as Americans, not sell them off to the highest bidder because they wish to stay in office. The time to stand up for the legacy of America is now! Should we not demand that our Country be preserved and respected for future generations instead of immediate gratification?

CHAPTER 24
MEDIA

I have always had a great respect for journalists. They spend their day reading, researching and interviewing subjects on various topics of interest. These artisans then transform their research into what we read or hear in our daily news reports. Unfortunately, this is not always the case.

For many years, I have seen the ugliest side of journalism while living in Washington, DC. Stories that have been fabricated way beyond comprehension from the original truth. I have seen people's lives destroyed by some of these stories, yet the media never stops. They seem to be predators thirsting for blood and destruction without any remorse. Mainstream media's objective to every story is to looks for "If it bleeds – It Leads" type stories, which are destructive to everyone.

When dealing with the war, they miss the unique opportunity to tell the whole story. Stories that tell of emotions and soul searching, loved ones, heroism and the ultimate sacrifice because they lack the sensational attraction of ratings boosts. They fail to tell these stories because it is not politically polarizing enough for public distribution.

Instead, they fight to report a story before obtaining the real facts behind the story. It is not rocket science to figure out the why in their actions. They rush the story in order to beat out the other networks and publications so they can claim credit for the scoop of the day.

Even before I went to Iraq, I knew something was not right with how our media was reporting our involvement in the war on terrorism, and our presence in Iraq or Afghanistan. Every story was like a piece of a puzzle; each piece showing only a glimpse into the truth. Unfortunately, we never got to see the truth being told. In our hectic lives, we never try to put the pieces together in order to see the whole story.

Upon my return, I began to put the pieces together, but the whole story had not revealed itself until I visited Vietnam.

After returning from the trip to Vietnam, I really began to wonder what was going on with our media. This is when I began doing some research into the history of media's reporting on various wars. I spoke to numerous veterans from as far back as WWII about the accuracy and portrayal of their war in the media. What I learned was earth shattering.

Prior to Vietnam, those who reported the facts were in uniform. They were called "war correspondents'" and they knew what price could be paid if they reported the story incorrectly. They also knew that if they said too much, they or their brothers would be wounded, tortured or unfortunately killed as a result. During Vietnam, it was different.

Vietnam had a new venue for news – television. This new venue and its affiliated stations wanted their reporters to report from the frontlines. Those reporters did not want to be there, so with this animosity they opposed it going and the war to an unusual extent. Their hostility toward their bosses colored their perceptions and feeling about the war, and eventually they resented the soldiers themselves.

Those in uniform would suffer by their words and actions. Many of the 600 reporters had no strength to endure the rigors of a battlefield. Only a select few were adventurous and went outside the limits to obtain the real stories. These were real journalists. The others would rather stay in the safe zones then tempt fate and die like so many of their fellow Americans at the hands of the enemy. Vietnam changed how we received news from a combat zone.

Television was a great invention for entertainment, but when it came to the news, it is a different story. The war was by all accounts, the first 'Reality Show.'

Throughout my journey in Vietnam, it was unmistakably clear that Hanoi proclaimed they could not have won the war if it were not for the cooperation of the Western media. To them, the words and pictures used by the western media helped forge a battle to be won over any modern weapons on the battlefield. They praised their triumph from television the most.

How could the American people support the war effort when they were seeing death and destruction while sitting on their couch or at the dinner table? The more dramatic the scenes were, the more the American people reacted. Burning villages and gruesome desecration of human beings were considered news worthy. A reporter never said or wrote that it cost him a carton of cigarettes, or it was his lighter that torched that building that stood burning behind him. The same reporter never said how he dared the unwary soldier to stage many of the fights portrayed behind him in these reports. Moreover, the words that were later used in these reports would cut into the heart of every service member when they learned how they were being portrayed back home. Without any military experience or background, these civilian reporters also gave personal comments and predictions on the outcome of the war.

I was appalled to learn of so many inaccuracies by selfish reporters with cravings of power and grandeur for the spotlight on the evening news back home. Reporters who went with political agendas already formulated without knowing the historical information of the battle at hand. Many lacked the experience to do an in depth report on the complexities of war, politics, international affairs, or what was right and wrong. With no integrity, these stories based on editors likes and dislikes were reported each night. Editors who held the strings of a reporter's career like a puppeteer in a new form of media - television.

The Art of Journalism Changed Forever.

As time went, on it became a contention of ideologies between the media and politicians, a battle fought on the pages of newspapers and television screens versus on the battlefield. Interestingly enough those who reported less than the truth were never near any real conflict of war in most cases. They were not on the DMZ where many Marines were losing their lives, but winning the battles before them. They were not in the highlands where the Army struggled daily. Where were they? They were in Saigon drinking with senior officers at the Rex Hotel – enjoying a lavish lifestyle while soldiers, Marines and airmen were suffering the hardships of a real war. The American people were not ready and never will be ready to fight a battle on television.

What was the result of their reports? Their reports created a society that bred only hatred and venom, which helped to dismantle the last vestiges of wavering respect for our Armed Forces that American people once had. The reporters had no respect or sympathy for those trying to survive and stay alive in the real war and they did not care if they reported it incorrectly.

Because of the irresponsibility of those reports, historians will never reflect the truth nor will history reflect that military battle between North Vietnamese guerilla fighters and both south Vietnamese and American forces was won militarily by the latter. Neither will it show how they destroyed guerilla fighters who infiltrated the south for reinforcements to fight for the north. No one reads that many of these reinforcements were captors, forced to fight for the guerilla fighters. Because of mainstream media's reporting from Saigon, political pressure in Washington wavered and they succumbed to pressure to withdraw support for the South Vietnamese. Historians neglected to focus the sham where it belonged on the politicians who caused the ultimate fall of Saigon, instead casting a broad net on all associated with the war, including a twisted and distorted shadow which disgraced those soldiers who fought and died bravely in the name of the United States of America.

Many of those who were in Vietnam to report will never admit to the perversions of the truth, yet they will continually blame those in Washington and that of Americas supposed failure. If one looks back at this time in history objectively, we can now see that ignorance of the political hierarchy played a major role in the sixties crusades that helped destroy the 'American Way of life.'

Vietnam was not lost due to military failure; it was lost in the minds of the American people due to political failure and psychological warfare. This psychological warfare propaganda undermined the overall advancements our Armed Forces were having on behalf of the Vietnamese people.

I can now understand why every single Vietnam veteran feels betrayed. Their fellow Americans, who were supposed to be telling their story to their families back home, had betrayed them.

When I began to look at the current war, I could to see similarities in how our media is reporting events. I compared them to reports I was receiving from those serving in Iraq or Afghanistan. They were very different from those I watched on the evening news or read in the paper. I began to wonder if it was only gross negligence in the facts, or was it being done for another reason.

I began to have major concerns about the media, even more after returning home from Iraq. I never saw the war they were portraying each night. The main question I came away with was what is causing all this destructive behavior in our media. Is it inadequate leadership? Is it political in nature? Was it just irresponsibility of the media, and reporting the facts incorrectly, or something more sinister? This last question truly bothered me. This is when I remembered something my father said when I was growing up: "The real truth is on the battlefield." Then he would mutter the phrase "Damn Propaganda." As a child, I did not know what this meant. I remembered coming home from the VFW, one Saturday afternoon in searched of the dictionary. I looked the word up and was more perplexed than before with its definition: "The systematic propagation of a given view or interest." Still baffled, I returned to my father with dictionary in hand asking what the definition and his statement meant.

As a career military officer, he explained it this way – "Propaganda during war or even in peace time is like advertising. Their advertising influences a person or group of people for a purpose, or in this case, the war, for the obvious self deception of an opinion or fact." He further explained it in political terms, "Politicians use propaganda much in the same way. They use arguments that sound as though they have value or merit, always sounding extremely convincing to a person who is too lazy to seek the truth and all the while the facts are invalid." He continued: "In war both sides use bits and pieces of the truth for their own self gain, while the real issues – those being fought on the battlefield are never reported. Because during war the average citizen can not handle the truth associated with war." He would then begin complaining about the media once again and would say that it was manipulative and irresponsible. "The media used to be responsible during war, knowing that what they reported could kill soldiers on the battlefield. In recent years, they have fallen short on their responsibilities. As a result, they inflate the truth for ratings, advertising dollars and personal gain of one's own career in television."

Although I was entrenched in the political arena here in Washington, DC, until this journey, I never understood the damage he referred to. As with anything in life, education is the key to unlocking the mysteries before our eyes. This journey unlocked the truth about how the media became the propaganda machine that is helping to destroy this nation. In today's war, they are helping to divide a nation in even more destructive ways than ever before.

As the pieces of the puzzle began to come together in my mind, more questions formed in my thoughts. I began searching to see if there was an oath of ethics for journalists that helps guide them in their reporting. Although there are many guidelines journalists follow, in speaking to one local reporter friend, he directed me to the list published in the "Elements of Journalism" by Bill Kovach and Tom Rosenstiel as a list of ethics to consider for this book. What I found was an oxymoron: (comments in brackets are my responses to these ethical standards)

1. Journalism's first obligation is to the truth. (*they rarely tell the whole truth*)

2. Its first loyalty is to the citizens. (*first loyalty is to their editors and advertisers*)

3. Its essence is discipline of verification. (*rarely do they verify data*)

4. Its practitioners must maintain an independence from those they cover. (*Politically motivated not independent*)

5. It must serve as an independent monitor of power. (*again politically motivated*)

6. It must provide a forum for public criticism and compromise. (*instead it instills fear and destroys reputations*)

7. It must strive to make the significant interesting and relevant. (*Keeps interest in a politically motivated story to help twist the facts to produce a different outcome*)

8. It must keep the news comprehensive and proportional. (*ONE SIDED REPORTING*)

9. Its practitioners must be allowed to exercise their personal conscience (*this also allows for personal political agendas as well*)

There was never a mention of 'Ethics, Integrity, or Character;' wonder why this is?

Although the First Amendment prohibits our government from dictating to the media, what it should and should not print, one key element came to the surface very quickly. The media is run by corporate America and it is corporate America who is dictating what the government can and will do. It is up to the editors of their respective outlets to select what they sensor. Editors help corporate America by fueling the fires of various programs that their corporate advertisers want pushed through Congress. At of this is at the expense of the American people, it is a very ugly game. It is a high stakes poker game where the stakes are much higher than any financial gain; it is being played at the cost of our freedom and liberty.

Forget about the war for a moment, lets look at the reports that were presented during and after Hurricane Katrina hit New Orleans in 2005. During Katrina, there were numerous reports of "not much damage in the area of the hurricane." It would be a few days before the country would learn just how irresponsible these reports were, and that the reporters gave this information without proper investigation and facts. As a result, critical aid and support was not immediately available to those who needed it the most. When a crisis occurs and our own media misreports the seriousness of a crisis, the situation clearly becomes more dangerous.

For example, one reporter reported that there was no significant damage in New Orleans. What he failed to report was that he was in the French Quarter. The French Quarter did not sustain any of the real harshness of the storm; therefore, he had an opportunity to report that he was not able to determine any other damage to the surrounding areas of the city. At the time of his report, the levy across town had already given way and caused significant flooding damage. Because of his blatant disregard, and lack of responsibility as a reporter, emergency assistance was not rendered fast enough to those who needed it. That one report had a domino effect and sent the situation into a dangerous spiral that caused many to perish as a result.

Meanwhile, another reporter claimed there were over 200 deaths at the Superdome, immediately following the hurricane. Later, we learned less than ten people actually died at the Superdome. These deaths were not from the hurricane, but from drug overdoses, natural causes and one suicide of a mentally ill individual. Here again the media had an opportunity to rally the world for assistance, instead they caused panic and hate. They even missed the stories of many civilian and military personnel who were rendering aid, selfless acts of bravery by those who were risking their own lives to save others. Instead, they distorted the truth to suit their own needs.

Meanwhile, each night we hear repeatedly that this has been the bloodiest month so far in Iraq. Damn I thought last month was the bloodiest. Do they even have a clue what a bloody month looks like? When the media reports the number of deaths associated with the war in Iraq, one has to question their facts. When they report a total number of deaths since the beginning of the war as 3480, you must understand that these deaths are not all from hostile encounters. As reflected in the following chart from the recently released Congressional Report presented to Congress in July 2007 of the American War and Military Operations Casualties; as you can see once the numbers are broken down there are other factors which are also in the numbers.

For example, the number of those killed in Action (hostile) was 2195 not the 3480 being reported. Included in this number are also accidents, illness, homicide and self-inflicted deaths. While these deaths are also a defining factor of being in a combat zone, there are many questions that need to be raised as to why they are being reported as they are. Take self-inflicted deaths, one has to ask why they took their own lives. Could it be because they were unstable to begin with? Maybe it was because they received a letter from a girlfriend or boyfriend breaking up with them. Could it have been because they could not live without their children who they lost at the hands of Child Protective Services just prior to their leaving for Iraq? As you can see, there are many factors that are not divulged in these reports. The following is a table produced in the Congressional report presented to Congress in September of 2007.

Table 13. Operation Iraqi Freedom, By Casualty Category Within Service, March 19, 2003, Through June 2, 2007

Casualty Type	Total	Army	Navy	Marines	Air Force
Killed in Action	2,193	1,497	51	626	19
Died of Wounds [a]	652	480	1	171	
Died While Missing In Action	7	7			
Died While Captured	2	2			
Total Hostile Deaths	2,854	1,986	52	797	19
Accident	405	279	10	106	10
Illness	63	53	7	2	1
Homicide	15	10	1	2	2
Self-Inflicted	113	96	3	14	
Undetermined	8	7	1		
Pending [b]	22	3	3	16	
Total Non-Hostile Deaths	626	448	25	140	13
Total Deaths	3,480	2,434	77	937	32
Total Wounded in Action	25,830	16,975	561	8,003	291
Total Medical Air Transported (Hostile and Non-Hostile)	34,778	28,418	987	4,126	1,247

Because of this kind of reporting, the average viewer cannot understand or comprehend what they are hearing. Reporters ask 'needless deaths are being taken for what?' If only they would step back and look at the bigger picture before them, would they cringe at their own ignorance?

The brave warriors who they disrespect with snide remarks like these, entered into a combat zone knowing the risk, and did so selflessly, without reservations.

Every time an American spouts off about needless deaths, they disrespect those who have put the uniform on. They not only disrespect those who gave the ultimate sacrifice, but they also disrespect their own legacy. They degrade the men and women who honorably serve in our Armed Forces who help safeguard them at home and around the world each day. They selfishly voice opinions about information they learn from the news only to realize later the news was very wrong. Do they go back to the people they spoke to and apologize? Never! To them they did nothing wrong. Why did they feel the information given to them was accurate? Is it because a reputable news program delivered the information to them? Believing propaganda equals ignorance and aids the enemy in their objectives.

If one looks at the bigger picture, they would be embarrassed to say a word. They would cringe at the thought of how hypocritical they have become. Take issues that can be controlled here at home that most people do nothing about. "Do you drink beer or alcohol?" Most do, so how many needless deaths occur each day by someone being stupid and driving drunk? Do they get on the news each night and report the needless deaths from this situation? No! How many drivers, drive on our roads recklessly? It is called road rage! How many needless deaths have to occurred because someone was to busy too pay attention and killed a person because they were in a hurry? The kicker in this query is this: one will bitch about the needless deaths of our Armed Forces for fighting for freedom, yet, they will not bitch about things that are affecting their lives around them. They will do nothing about drunk driving, crime in our neighborhoods, gang violence, drug dealers or needless accidents, which they themselves have control over. Instead, they will disrespect those who valiantly serve in our Army,

Navy, Air Force, Marines and Coast Guard for what they do. How hypocritical.

While our warriors seem to know the history of America, many Americans do not. Why is that? All one needs to do is watch television to see talk show hosts query people on the streets. The result will tell you how uneducated people are. Many do not know the names of our Presidents, Congress, Senators or even their Governors, much less know about the founding fathers and the history of their own country. This reality truly saddens me because unless one knows the history of their own country, they truly cannot speak about its future, or even the present with any clarity of understanding. In today's society, we spout off that we think we know what is happening in the world just because we watch the news!

Please understand that most of the news these days is propaganda and should seriously be questioned for its accuracy and content. In the fight against terrorism, you continually see fighting in Baghdad, Ramadi and Fallujah, so what is this doing for the war on terrorism? Nothing! All it does is create a venue for insurgents to display their handy work on the television. Most of what you see on the evening news happened that morning, before eleven o'clock Baghdad time. Insurgents know how to use our media just the way Hanoi used it back during Vietnam. If the media continually reports only the bad, guess what, we will continually feed the enemy the fuel on they crave to fire continued attacks and recruit additional insurgents. What a mistake!

Our media has an opportunity to change this situation by showing the accomplishments of those who are serving over in Iraq, yet they will never listen to me on this subject, maybe they will listen to you? Contact your local television station and newspaper and demand that they report the news more accurately. Tell them you are fed up with all the negativity they breed and you want them to report about the heroism on your streets at home and around the world. News reports should be about the good, not just the bad each day.

In Iraq, I was able to join two units of the United States Marine Corps on many convoys that took us to many places that mainstream media never visits. Media believes there is no news in that region. That region of Iraq is the forgotten territory. It is not the green zone, where they can play video games, feel safe and where all amenities of life are apparent. They do not have shops to frequent for souvenirs for loved ones and coworkers. That is because there is no fifteen minutes of fame in the area where I was. There are no bombs exploding every five seconds as one would believe by watching the news and rarely do you see an IED. Do not get me wrong they are always on the roads.

The green zone in Baghdad is much like it was back in Saigon. Many in the media never venture out of the green zone. It is much easier for them to wait for the feeds to come in from the combat photographers so they can build a story around the images.

While there are many successes throughout the country, there are some areas where the insurgents are still causing trouble. In the Al Anbar Province, the local Iraqi people are now policing the area, and it is semi-secured. You see, mainstream media only looks for the negative stories to exploit, rarely do they report on the wonderful successes our military and coalition forces are accomplishing every day. Unless they are used as fodder in a story, you will never hear of the places we visited on your evening news or in the newspaper. They do not dare visit the area because to them there is no news, except humanitarian news. These types of stories do not lead on your nightly news programs. This is because there is no blood being shed every five seconds. Remember, "If it bleeds – it leads." Therefore, you will never know of the many accomplishments. If one were to ask any reporter who visited Iraq, "Is progress being made in combating terrorism or are humanitarian efforts being achieved in Iraq?" Most would say yes to both, and their eyes will light up as they tell you about a school, hospital or some other form of humanitarian story. However, if you further asked them why they were not reporting this information in their articles or reports, they would simply answer as their editors and producers would tell them... "That doesn't sell newspapers or get us ratings time." Where is the ethics and integrity in journalism these days?

Instead of showing the successes of our military forces for capturing caches of weapons and helping to rebuild water treatment plants, electrical plants and vital infrastructure, they are scorned in news reports. They will never be mentioned for helping to save human lives by providing medical treatment and supplies. You will never hear the stories of how the Army, Navy and Marines have helped save animals at the zoo in Baghdad. You do not hear the story of a group of National Guard Soldiers who obtained a wheelchair for a child who could not walk because of deformed feet. You will never hear the stories of how these same warriors delivered babies in the middle of the night, or pooled their own money and resources to fly a child to the United States for special surgery that saved their lives.

Our media would rather play politics with the lives of our brothers, sisters, nieces, nephews, husbands and wives then to report the truth. While the media plays politics using our military as fodder in their reports during war, they are aiding the enemy. This is a form of treason, which is dangerous and deadly to those in uniform.

I can now say without a doubt, the media can take credit for many casualties, both during Vietnam and in the war in Iraq. Their bias and inaccurate reporting skills of war are a direct result of their irresponsibility in using politics to promote fear and distain for those in uniform. Corporate America should be ashamed at how they manipulate the media to control those in government.

CHAPTER 25
POLITICS VS. WAR

Politics and power is a drug all its own! The more an elected official craves it, the more addicted they become to it.

If our elected officials would only look back into our own history, they could learn from their predecessors' achievements and gain valuable lessons on their subsequent failures. Unfortunately, instead of learning from the past in order to forge a better tomorrow, they continually repeat the same mistakes as if they were newfound ideas. They continually capitalize on the pain of past mistakes and infest the minds of our fellow Americans with the horror of their rival party's mistakes. As a result, we see how political power and subsequent greed rears its ugly head more often than it has united us.

Our elected officials deceived us after September 11, 2001, when they gathered on the steps of the Capitol Building and joined hands. That day they pledged, while holding hands, to work together in a non-partisan way to defend America at all costs. I was inspired at their action and I was not alone. Many Americans thought it was a wake up call for them to work together, as one body of government, but so soon, they forgot. It only took six short months for them to forget their own pledge, before they were again at each other's throats. I guess they missed those fifteen minutes of spotlight each night on the evening news.

Many will read this chapter and think oh this woman is a republican or a democrat by the way she speaks. Many will say I am writing this book because I am a pro-war activist, which is why I speak the way I do. I am sorry to disappoint you on both these statements. I am but one American who can look at many factors, based on the evidence then draw my own conclusion and answer. Accordingly, just for the record, I do not belong to any political party - I am only an American.

My Father, who was very politically active, taught me to look at both sides of every issue, "Gather the evidence and then after reviewing the evidence form your own conclusion." He would then continue, "That conclusion must be based on one important factor - what the Declaration of Independence and Constitution says – only then can you make an informed decision." Because I make my mind about an issue after considering all the evidence and facts, coupled with what my heart and conscience tells me is the right thing to do, his formula works for me.

Many times over, it has gotten me into trouble with both political parties here in DC. Other times it has changed the way people look at an issue as well. While most in Washington believe that you should tote the party line, many here in town understand that I am not one to tote the political correctness line both because I am not affiliated with either party and because I am not politically correct by any means. I will be the first to challenge them on issues and bring the evidence and facts before them in order for them to form their own conclusion. By doing this, I also challenge them as my elected officials to do what is right for the American People. I am now the first to denounce them when they tote that party line because they have sold their souls to the sharks on Capitol Hill.

It is very clear when you consider the evidence being presented to us that there needs to be a complete change on Capitol Hill in the upcoming elections. Both House and Senate need to be cleaned out completely. Let me give you a few examples as to why I suggest this. Elected officials in Washington look at the War on Terrorism much as they do on the war on poverty, drugs, crime and healthcare. They will ignore these issues unless they can further their own political agenda and gain yet another fifteen minutes of fame before any willing television camera.

If you have watched the news this past year, I bet you have cringed just as much as I have. While some elected officials have the maturity to be a representative, others who are suppose to be so-called adults, will stand before the world in the House of Representatives fighting and acting like children in kindergarten. Even children in kindergarten are not allowed to act that way. They have been taught to have much more respect for each other than these men and woman do. Of course, Congress and the House don't have a kindergarten teacher there to arbitrate. These are the Senators and Congressional representatives that are representing us before the world - this is embarrassing.

Over the years, books about the political side war have failed to tell the most important story of all; words spoken by political representatives can either win a war, or kill Americans on the battlefield. When it is not for their own personal gain, they are all for sending troops in to bring stability to a country or region.

Yet when they are running for reelection or higher office, they will change their stand on a subject in order to suit their own needs. In searching for a few political speeches and comments to show this point, I was surprised to fall upon many speeches that jumped out at me. One such speech said it all, and was delivered by a man I admire greatly - Robert F. Kennedy.

It was during the Vietnam War and he was running for the Presidency against Johnson.

It was only three years prior to that election he thought the involvement of American forces in Vietnam was the right thing to do for liberty and freedom. Unfortunately, during his own political campaign for the Presidency, he denounced our involvement and uttered the words that stung my heart as I read his words. These words along with others of the day helped divide us as a nation – *"This is an un-winnable war."* Robert F. Kennedy. I could not believe that he of all people would change his tune for political gain.

In recent years, many of our current day politicians have done similar things. When high-ranking Senators and Congressmen use their position to undermine the mindset of the public and the President of the United States it is dangerous for our National Security. Case in point; Congresswoman Nancy Pelosi was cautioned and advised by the National Security

Counsel, Department of Defense, State Department and the President of the United States to not enter into Syria, yet she took it upon herself to thumb her nose at all who were better qualified than she is and flew to Syria for a meeting.

Congresswoman Pelosi is one of the first representatives on the Hill to complain about military spending. Then why does she utilize a USAF 757 for her air travel back and forth from DC to California? Why did she utilize this same USAF 757, and its crew to fly to Syria? By the way, she did not travel alone on that trip. She took with her members of her staff, bodyguards, and other military personnel who were part of the crew for the USAF 757. When we take into account the costs of fuel, manpower, per diem, hotel costs, danger to the troops, payroll, etc, one has to wonder where her power trip is coming from. She not only costs the taxpayers unnecessarily, but she has the nerve to bash our military and her opposition at every turn. She complains about waste, fraud and the expense of the war, yet she adds to that waste when she takes trips that she has no need of taking. Never does she mention the amount of waste she and other elected officials are racking up with their many trips overseas and how much those trips costs the taxpayer.

She also did not take into account that the men who she met with had no respect for her because she is a female. When is she going to understand that what ever was said to her; promises that were made are never going to come to fruition? In that culture, they do not take a woman seriously, nor do they take their advice. For an intelligent woman, she is very ignorant and full of herself thinking she has so much power outside of the United States. Either she is on an ego trip, or she hates America so much that she does not care what damage she does to it with her actions. It is entirely all about her!

When elected representatives enter Iraq to see what is happening, they never leave the green zone. They never see the real accomplishments, nor are they ever near the real combat zone. They only see the senior brass and the media on these trips. Therefore, they return home with the same "without a clue expression" on their face about the war. They get what is called; "the dog and pony show" that is given to guests. They travel with an entourage of bodyguards, press and staff that costs the taxpayers heavy-duty bucks, yet they never see the real deal. These trips are nothing more than an interruptive nuisance. Every military person within a fifty-mile radius of the green zone knows they are only there for their own ego; not to help them win the war by providing them with the much needed equipment and personnel. With the exception of a select few, who have returned home, lived up to their offers to help the troops, there is no real respect for any elected official that ventures into Iraq.

I have been very disappointed hearing Senator Harry Reid, Senator John Warner, Congressman John Murtha and many others blatantly disrespect those in the uniform. It is insulting to those who wear the uniform of our Armed Forces to hear someone who once wore the uniform denounce them. Have they forgotten what it is like to be in a combat zone? They should know better than anyone how that knife feels being thrust into your heart when you hear those who sent you into that war zone, say what you are doing is not worthy of our respect. It is even worse when you hear the words coming from a former veteran, "this is an unwinnable war." Comments like this tell me that these men are only in office for their own egos and should seriously retire because they have ceased representing the United States of America. They are representing themselves and their own personal agendas. They are representing their political party and not the American people any longer. They think only about themselves not about the future of this country, or the American citizens they were elected to represent.

We saw this type of disregard toward our fellow Americans when we watched the unfolding of the emergency management procedures during Hurricane Katrina. The Governor of Louisiana, together with the Mayor of New Orleans, refused assistance from the President of the United States because he was a republican and they were both democrats. Not only is this completely incompetent emergency management, but it goes to show you how deep party politics will go. They were both more interested in saving their future political careers rather than looking at the bigger picture.

When a politician is more concerned with party politics and career over the well-being of their fellow citizens, there is something gravely wrong. Governor Blanco of Louisiana repeatedly was offered assistance by the President prior to the hurricane hitting that area, but turned it down. It is very sad when First responders have to call friends in other states to beg for help during a crisis, only to find out later that help was turned away at the state line. The Governor turned it away claiming it was a liability. The help was redirected to Mississippi and was received with open arms.

In the aftermath of the storm, Governor Blanco again turned down offers of help by the administration. Why would any Governor turn down assistance from any federal agency during a crisis? One has to wonder what could motivate them to do such a thing.

It is very dangerous when a Governor feels they should play party politics during a crisis and turn down assistance for the people of their state. These actions resulted in not receiving the aid and comfort that is vital for survival. Governor Blanco should have been thrown out of office immediately, because of her gross negligence in handling that crisis. Was she more concerned about her political career than to accept help from anyone? That is a question only she can answer before God himself.

Later when called before a Senate Committee to discuss the breakdown of the emergency, Mr. Michael Brown accused Governor Blanco of being negligent in her handling of the situation. Instead of defending herself before the Committee, Governor Blanco refused to speak about her involvement in the crisis and said she would rather speak about job opportunities. Even her fellow Democrats on the committee were shocked at her response. Is she that ignorant, or, just that incompetent?

Mayor Ron Nagin is a whole other story in itself. Here is a bright intelligent executive who owns and runs a cable company in the New Orleans area. During an emergency crisis, he was more interested in playing the race card than doing his job effectively. New Orleans is in the path of these types of storms every year, why had he not ensured that his city have an effective emergency plan in the event of such a storm. Did he listen to his Director of Emergency Management during the Katrina Crisis to utilize the school buses to help evacuate those who could not get out of the dangerous zones? NO! Did he ever listen to his first responder teams who said they needed a new communication system that did not require landline connections in the event of a disaster? NO! Question is, was he more interested in creating new and exciting casinos and hotels for his city – in the flood zone of Wards that were flooded? Maybe he should look on his desk for the answer to that question.

Behavior such as this is not only dangerous; it seems to be the norm throughout the country. A politician does something negligent and the people of the community continue to reelect them back into office. What is wrong with this picture? Have voters lost perspective on what is right and wrong? We should not be rewarding these people with another term in office as a reward for being stupid, we should be treating them like criminals.

Just like Blanco and Nagin, representatives in Congress and Senate were the same way. They were more interested in slinging political dirt at not only the President but also thousands of others instead of closing their mouths and sending assistance to those who needed it the most. Each of them could have generated so much support and assistance if only they utilized their fifteen minutes to do something good; instead, they had their fifteen minutes of fame before the cameras so that their constituents could be proud of them. It was about them and not the American people who needed their help. As an American citizen, I was appalled at their behavior. When will they learn that the world is watching them just as we are?

Political Complacency Makes for Stupidity

Politicians are master artisans. Like actors, they will exploit an issue to rile a voter's emotion on a subject, just to get them to the polls to vote for them. It is called deception.

When I hear them say, "I support the troops, but not the War" my immediate response is, "I support the war, but not the troops." Now go back and reread what I just wrote please, then come back and tell me that statement does not sounded stupid. Yes it does. I respond this way to those on the street when they make the same statement. When they have that perplexed look come over their face, I immediately respond with, "That sounded stupid, didn't it?" Their response is always the same. "Yes it did." This is usually when I make a bolder comment, "Sounded just as stupid as what you just said. You see, you cannot have it both ways. You cannot support the troops and not the mission. You either support them both or do not send them into battle. This is not a walk around the block, sending troops into battle is a serious business. If you are not going to support your fellow Americans on the battlefield then you are not a true American."

At a time when our country should be uniting for the greater good of our national security, it continually repeats history. Unity should be the number one issue on the campaign trail in any election cycle, for we have American Military fighting a war in a foreign land. Every political candidate has the capability to encourage every American to be supportive of those who chose to put on the uniform of our country in the Army, Navy, Air Force, Marine Corps and Coast Guard. These men and woman are putting their lives at risk on a daily basis in foreign countries, under our flag. Instead, the politicians who are supposed to set the example for all of us to follow open their mouth and say something stupid to help further divide us.

Take for example Senator John Kerry (D-MA) who delivered a speech to students in California where he stated: "those unable to navigate the country's education system get stuck in Iraq." That one statement sent a clear message to everyone in the world how little our representatives think of our military. A statement coming from a man who won three purple hearts during Vietnam, but he failed to tell the students he inflicted those injuries on himself and wrote the paperwork up for those purple hearts. Talk about stupidity. But then again he is a college graduate after all; maybe he knows something they do not know.

Ignorance in our politicians is running rampant in Washington, DC. Maybe they do not know or understand that our military is hardly uneducated. On the contrary, they are extremely educated. Let me educate our elected officials here and their seemingly uneducated staff – many of whom do not even know the difference between the uniforms of the Armed Forces. Unlike those in politics, Soldiers, Sailors, Airman, Marines or Coast Guardsman's serve because they love this country not because of materialistic rewards for their service to their country. They serve because they feel in their hearts that it is right for them and most of all because they have honor, integrity, and character. Many on Capitol Hill have no honor, integrity, or character therefore; they do not know it when they see it.

Ninety-seven percent of the officers Corps in the military hold a degree of some kind, many hold a Masters Degree. Did you know about 40% of our enlisted service members hold a minimum of a bachelor's degree while the other 60% are taking courses to either gain that same bachelor's degree, or aspire to do the same? I personally have a number of family members in the service of our country at this time, five of which are West Point Graduates to be exact, as well as many friends who are serving with them who are just as educated.

I am amazed at times when people who are public officials, fail to think before they open their mouth. Did Senator Kerry not read that speech before he made it? When I watched the tape and listened to his speech, I could hear my father repeating his golden rule from the military. A rule he instilled in each of his kids and used in his own political life; "Think, Decide and Act. Think before you open your mouth or do something. Decide if the ramifications of your actions are going to harm yourself, those around you, or the nation as a whole. Only then act, but remember that your actions will always have ramifications. Most importantly, be ready to stand firm in your decision."

Senator Kerry's father served during World War II as my father did. I wonder if Senator Kerry thought about how his comments would fall on his father's ears if he were sitting in the audience that day. Did he think about how his father would feel, if he were sitting in a cockpit of one of his B-29 hearing such a thing from a politician in Washington DC during World War II? Apparently, he failed to remember that those kinds of negative messages delivered by politicians during the Vietnam War had a direct affect on those serving in the jungles of Vietnam. How those types of messages helped to perpetuate distain for our military in the minds of the American People. How that distain continues to foster stupidity every day. I guess he forgot how he felt while serving in uniform during a time of war, the feelings of betrayal by those political figures in positions of authority for their similar comments and actions that resulted in the derogation and embarrassment such as his. Now he is the one who is in the position of power doing the damage to the image of our troops. How soon they forget.

Because of the modern media, politicians, disrespect for the sacrifices of our military personnel who are in a combat zone can have an immediate impact on a soldier and even cost them their lives on the battlefield. How soon they forget once they get into political office and are given all that power. They fail to remember their responsibility to the American people when it is more important to get their names in the paper for that next election. It is sad how history repeats itself by the same characters that screamed and yelled at Congress for betraying them during a time of war.

Are we destined to follow the Romans, as in the fall of the Roman Empire, where the power and greed of their leaders destroyed their society because they could not govern their own daily lives? Are we destined to continue to see the struggles of good versus evil because no one is doing anything to stop the evil? Should we continue to witness unnecessary legislation enacted, that will ultimately cause harm in the future? Are we to continue to incarcerate the innocent and allow criminals to walk the streets?

Politics can be a very dangerous game when those in power feel they are elitists, self-serving representatives that have lost sight of the fact they were elected by the people and for the people. They feel they are above the interest of the common person because they hold a degree from some university. We know we are in serious trouble especially when they argue they should not have to answer for their indiscretions. This universal character flaw in our politicos needs to be changed.

I think it is time to search our souls before we vote in future elections. We need to ask ourselves, where is the leadership? Where is the leadership from those who want to become our leaders? Everyone wants to step up and get the job, but who is stepping up with something that would make us want to follow him or her? As in every campaign in history, they are no different. When a candidate has no clear objective plan for any issue, they resort to the old school mentality of the character assassination of their opponents. In future elections, I want you to consider a few key elements before surrendering your vote for any one candidate. Where are the leaders we are to elect that have a well thought out plan for change in immigration violations, economic reform, cleaning up government waste, or holding those in public office accountable for their lack of respect and ethics violations on Capitol Hill. Better yet National Security issues; a clear plan to bring Korea, Iran, Iraq, Afghanistan, terrorism or crime under control to safeguard America's real interests and security. If we are not willing to accept the political propaganda from our government, then why are we willing to accept it from our respected political parties who want to lead us in the same government? Americans need to wake up and become better educated on the issues at hand. Do not take what your political party dishes out as the solemn truth.

A person in public office who wishes to stand before their fellow Americans, and make stupid statements, a joke or not, does not deserve to be elected into office. I have no respect for any elected official who is not willing to adhere to the following rules of etiquette as my elected representative.

Rules of Etiquette for Elected Officials.

1) Speak publicly on issues before you in Congress.
2) Speak publicly about the concerns of every American, for you represent every American while in elected office, not just your home district.
3) Set an example for citizens of our country to follow:

serving with character, honesty, integrity, morality and patriotism

4) You have a responsibility to safeguard unity, patriotism and most of all the foundation of American values. These values include service to our country in uniform of the armed forces. This responsibility does not give you the right to degrade those who have, are, or will serve in that uniform for future generations.

5) Most of all remember that when you open your mouth in public or in private, you represent me and my fellow Americans – be careful of what you say, because those that are the enemy of our country are surely listening to what is said and could ultimately cause us all harm based on your actions and words.

I think those who have taken up permanent residency on Capitol Hill have become complacent and need to think about retiring. I think it's time that the system be changed to term limits, maybe then we might be able to choose leaders who will truly represent the people. Then maybe, just maybe, we might have leadership worth respecting?

For those who received your seats in Congress or Senate based on family name, you are not true servants of the people. You are nothing more than tokens for the people who are paying for that seat. You have sold your souls to the lobbyists, corporate America and special interest groups to be their voice and nothing else. You are the people who are the most dangerous, because you are willing to sell out this country for a buck, rather than serve honorably in the footsteps of our founding fathers intention of what a member of the House of Representatives was supposed to be.

The founding fathers did not serve based on monetary rewards, pensions or benefits. They served because they loved this country and everything it represents – FREEDOM!

Benjamin Franklin writing as Silence Dogood once said, "Without Freedom of Thought, there can be no such Thing as Wisdom; and no such Thing as publick Liberty, without Freedom of Speech; which is the Right of every Man... This sacred Privilege is so essential to free Governments, that the Security of Property, and the Freedom of Speech always go together; and in those wretched Countries where a Man cannot call his Tongue his own, he can scarce call any Thing else his own. Whoever would overthrow the Liberty of a Nation, must begin by subduing the Freeness of Speech; a Thing terrible to Publick Traytors." The New-England Courant, July 9, 1722.

Mr. Franklin was accurate in his statement. Therefore, we must not allow the mistakes of the past to reap their ugly head once again. We must look to ourselves rather than to our leaders for answers. We must ask ourselves many questions. Have we become complacent in our thoughts about our country and this war? Have we become so materialistic that we are blinded by reality? Have we become so self-absorbed that we do not see what is happening around us, how special interest groups and politicians are manipulating us? Have we hidden ourselves in our homes, rather than admit there is an evil knocking at our doors and in our communities? Do we really need to be that affluent that we fail to see that our economy is spinning into an abyss.

Politicians say it is because of bad leadership in the White House. Others say it is a sign of a different world. Some say it is because of the war in the Middle East. I see it as three individual indicators that are causing the major problems within our society, indicators that every American has the power to change.

1) Smoke and Mirror Politicians:

In the political arena smoke and mirror politicians raise issues that get a candidate immediate press; such as Roe v. Wade, gun rights and gay rights. A candidate will raise these issues if he or she has no real platform to stand on. When a candidate brings up these issues, this should tell you they are a token candidate for their political party. Their political party does not have a real leader within their ranks to represent you in office. Political parties know that the voter is uneducated when it comes to issues. This allows them to entice you to vote for their token candidate so they will have control over you in that office. The world sits and watches as we struggle with the thought of losing everything we hold precious in our lives, as the political wars begin, what will you do to stop it?

2) Bait and Switch Issue

The environment should be a key issue to all who live on this planet, but we should look closely at those who are delivering the message.

Many of those who are on the bandwagon of the environmental issues have personal investments in the outcome if this issue. These are the very people you should be concerned about because they speak out of both sides of their mouth. On one hand, they say cut the defense budget to ensure that war-fighting capabilities are halted in the war effort. What they do not understand is that every time we cut the defense budget, we cut funding for the environment.

The Department of Defense is the largest environmental program in this country. On a daily basis, they are the leaders in environmental resource management, conservation and education, on U.S. military bases here at home and throughout the world. Funding from DoD helps to support colleges, technical schools and students in education and research projects that help the environment. Those who receive their PhD and Masters degrees in most cases have done their internship on a military installation or through a Defense Department funded project. These projects concentrate on our life in and around waterways and streams, land use, conservation and clean up, air purification capabilities, rescuing and safeguarding animals and endangered species.

Who will benefit the most if we are to convert to electric vehicles? It will not be the car dealers directly. Who is the leader in the environmental issue these days? Who will benefit from laws enacted to ensure cleaner air? Will it be one man or a group of people that lead the fight?

It surely will not be the citizens of the United States or even the world, because someone always has their hands in the pocket of someone who controls the money at some point. We the people should take a stronger, active role in saving our environment because we live her. We as a people should be more responsible in our efforts to recycle and conserve wherever we can. This issue doesn't just affect us; it affects the future of our children.

3) Economic Destruction Issue:

Now we have the major issue that most directly affects us all, the economic issue. We have those who control the very essence of our economy; he was a man who could cause the stock market and other indicators to going into a tailspin, Alan Greenspan! This man had been out of touch with reality for many years prior to stepping down, yet for many years prior to his replacement the stock market reacted violently any time he sneezed! Reality is that our economy is now feeling the full effects of the attack of September 11.This was the goal and objective of the terrorists from the beginning, destroy the economic well-being of the strongest country in the world. As with recent events in our economic status, they have begun to succeed.

Instead of our financial leaders advising and encouraging Corporate America to reinvest in the American People, Corporate America is looking at their bottom line. Corporate America undoubtedly has been thinking incorrectly. Instead of investing in their employees as if, they are their private stock market, they listened to Greenspan. One has to wonder what would happen if they changed their mentality of the stock market being a better investment than a loyal employee! Companies wonder why they are continually sabotaged, if only they would look at themselves and how they conduct business with their own employees. Corporate sabotage results in other people losing their jobs and the income that supports their family.

One of the basic lessons in any business course is when a company is in a slump, that's when you need to reinvest in that company, reevaluate its past performance and modify, as needed its policy, practices and results. For some strange reason companies are not doing this. Is it because our thought process is so turned around, we cannot think about business ethics, but rather focus on always making money? We need to start thinking about reinvesting in our own companies, from the top down. Presidents and CEO's should voluntarily not resign that leased vehicle agreement in favor of driving their own vehicle. As would any good leader, they should consider setting the example by making the same sacrifices their employees are being asked to make... such as cutting back expenses for any unnecessary items until things turn around. Leading by example retains loyal employees and creates a cohesive team willing to weather the storm and help strengthen the company in the future. This also ensures confidence in consumer loyalty as well. If Corporate America thought properly, they would know that this is the time to reinvest in this country and the people who helped make them rich.

Before I close this chapter, one last thing, Politicians who think they can run a war, from behind a desk on Capitol Hill, are in fantasyland. Many are career politicians who are not capable of properly running for reelection; especially when they are re-elected based on a legacy or family name. If they can't do the basic functions of their own jobs, they should leave war fighting to those who have been trained for it - our Armed Forces.

CHAPTER 26
JOURNEY TO VIETNAM
THE PRESENT BEGINS TO REVEAL
A PAST LONG FORGOTTEN

"Learn from the past and forge a better tomorrow"

A few weeks after returning home from Iraq, I boarded a plane heading west towards Vietnam. My traveling partners on this trip were not like my previous companions, yet they are still the same in their hearts. This group of United States Marines served in Vietnam over almost forty years ago.

This journey would be like no other I have ever taken in my travels. In the few weeks before embarking on this phase of my journey, I spent long hours at the National Archives, going through old pictures of the places on my itinerary. I familiarized myself with what it looked like during the war. Although I had seen many of the same photographs over the last few years, I was now looking at them with different eyes. I began to get a sense of another type of combat zone. A combat zone unlike the one I had left only a few short weeks before. I noticed things I had never noticed before. A strange feeling came over me with each photograph. A new understanding of these men began to emerge because of my experience in Iraq.

Vietnam Veterans are a different breed of men. Many in today's society describe them as rough, tough, bitter old men who cannot let go of the past. Society branded these brave warriors as baby killers, suicide mongers, drug addicts and alcoholics upon their return home, but they are none of these things.

We landed at Tan Son Nhut Airport just on the outside of Ho Chi Minh City, the former capitol city once known as Saigon. Now a major airport, it was once a strategic airbase back in the sixties. The weather was the complete opposite from what I had just left in Iraq. From the moment we stepped off the plane, we were soaked in sweat from the heat and humidity.

A city of chaotic traffic, motorbikes, mopeds and cyclos fill the street. Temples and pagodas are everywhere. Women were not dressed as exotically as I thought; instead, they were a mix of western clothing and the traditional Ao-dais. High-rise buildings line the skyline just as markets lined the streets.

Our hotel was in the heart of the old city, near the Rex Hotel and former French Palace. Normally I would have written down interesting tidbits for a travel article, but tourism wasn't my focus on this trip. The presence of my companions took my thoughts in another direction.

I walked along the streets of the city and was amazed at how much it changed while still holding on to its historical past. The Rex Hotel was not far and as I approached the building with its bright lights, I began to wander back to the pictures I had seen at the Archives.

The Rex Hotel was the command center, housing and chow hall for high-ranking officers and western media during the Vietnam War. It was the Green Zone, or safety zone, far away from the bombs and bullets. As I sat at a table in the rooftop bar, I looked out over the city and tried to imagine life during the war. Senior officers and media representatives sharing drinks and cigars, laughing at each other's jokes while fellow Americans were fighting for their lives in the jungles. The more I sat there thinking about the vision that was forming in my mind, the more I became angry at their callousness.

When I left the hotel, I walked towards the French Palace at the end of the road and found myself standing before a statute of Ho Chi Minh. The oddness of its location, and the eerie smile upon his face seemed to make a statement of satisfaction and accomplishment.

The next morning we headed towards the Mekong Delta and the Chu Chi Tunnels. I walked along the trails in the wooded area around the tunnels and could hear the crackling of branches under someone's feet. Insects, worms and animals scurried to get out of our way, and my skin began to crawl imagining these things crawling on me. I looked at the trunks of old trees and saw remnants of what could have been bullet holes buried into their flesh and bark. There was medium size bowl shape pits covered with new foliage in the floor of the landscape that were reminders of bombs dropped long ago.

Life is quite different than it was long ago. Exploding bombs that once blanketed the landscape have been replaced by thunderclouds on a rainy afternoon. Sounds of honking motorbikes have replaced the rat-tat tat of bullets that echoed alongside the rice patties lining the roads. Wind rustling through the elephant grass has replaced the footsteps of the enemy. Roads and bridges have been re-built. People's lives have carried on, but the memories are still there. For the warriors I travel with, memories that once were suppressed all these years, begin to make their way to the surface.

Our guide began to show us various openings to the tunnels while describing life underground. My thoughts immediately rushed to our military and those they called "Tunnel Rats." Thoughts of them climbing down into these cavernous tunnels, crawling on their bellies seeking out the enemy, my heart began to race. The thought of their being below ground for any length of time and the possibility of a bomb exploding above them, began to suck the air out of my lungs. Seeing these tunnels, I now understood why so many of them have claustrophobia.

A short time later, while climbing onto a boat for a ride across the Mekong River, a photograph of the area flashed through my mind. The picture was filled with small and medium sized boats of the U.S. Navy that once inhabited this area during the war; their mission was to secure the area from large and small boats bringing in supplies to the guerillas of the Viet Cong. I looked out over the dirty water as we slowly crossed the river, trying to imagine the Navy's patrol boats as they struggled to control this vital area of the south.

Once on the other side, I felt as though I was crossing a line into the unknown when we stepped into a canoe style boat and began quietly wadding through a small waterway under a canapé of bamboo grass. The quietness of the narrow river, shielded by the tall grass above me, gave me an uneasy feeling.

I felt like a predator approaching its prey. When the mouth of the river flowed out onto the Mekong, I realized the intensity of that short trip. This was how they snuck up on our warriors in the stillness of the night.

When we arrived back in Saigon, I quietly reviewed the pictures I had captured at the Archives before setting off exploring Saigon. I ventured over to Tu Do Street, a place known to enlisted wary soldiers for cheap saloons and female companions. It was no longer dirty and run down, but invaded by high priced fashion shops. I walked down the street feeling as though I had walked into Georgetown or Los Angeles. Signs for Gucci, Prada and Halston were visible everywhere; what a difference forty years has made to this economy.

While I walked along the streets in the heart of Saigon, I tried to imagine life back during the war. I tried to picture a young soldier, rushing down the street to get vital information to some General, who was drinking his scotch above the Rex Hotel. As I walked past an outdoor café, I could see those of the western media sitting at one of the tables sipping coffee, while they waited for dispatches to come in from the battlefield. Maybe they were reading the headlines of a newspaper, dreaming of the day their name would appear in that byline. The thought began to make me sick.

When we left Saigon and flew north towards Da Nang, I peered out the window at the landscape below. I was flying above an area the United States Army defended during the war. In 1970 Ray was stationed somewhere down there. I watched the valleys and mountains below me slowly move away; knowing that Binh Dinh Province and LZ Uplift was somewhere down there and said a silent prayer. I vowed to one-day visit that area.

When the plane began its decent, I looked out the window once again. I was surprised to see all the revetments, concrete bunkers and hangers that Marines once used. Da Nang airport during the war was a Marine Corps strategic air base.

Almost immediately, I felt a difference in the air and in the men in my group. I gingerly asked one man, who was once stationed at the base, how it felt to be back here, after all this time. "Strange," he said. "I worked in the next building. These buildings were all hangers back then." He added. Then he went silent and I could see in his eyes, he was reminiscing. I watched him for a few moments and could see his face beginning to change. I knew the ghosts were approaching the door. For a brief moment, I wondered if he regretted coming on this trip, just then his smile slowly began to return. He looked over at me and winked.

Not far from Da Nang Air base is a place called China Beach. A strip of golden sandy beach, where military personnel relieved stress from the hell of combat life. We arrived at China Beach I noticed something take hold of these men, a distant memory of purpose and determination. Their smiles said it all as they walked towards the waters edge. They began to change before my very eyes, from men in their mid-fifties to the young, vibrant men of their youth. I stood watching as they plunged into the surf of the South China Sea, laughing and splashing each other, and I could not help but smile.

While they frolicked in the surf, I took off my sandals and began walking along the sandy beach, allowing the water to cool off my feet. Pictures of military personal relaxing in the sun, or playing football and volleyball filled my mind. With each face I remembered those bright smiles upon their faces I wondered how many of those smiling faces become a casualty of war. My eyes began to fill up with tears thinking of the many horrors released on this very beach.

The next day we ventured south to Hoi An. In the dew of the morning, I noticed the landscape beneath my window as the sun was coming up over the horizon, and there were rice paddies for as far as the eye could see and the tranquil Thu Bon River to my right. I knew the area had seen heavy fighting during the war, but it was hard to imagine anything disrupting the beautiful sight I was now seeing.

The country is at peace, but is still hotter than hell. The humidity was overwhelming at times and I began to miss the dry heat of Iraq.

We made our way north towards Hue along Route 1. Once a dirt road that carried our troops, both Route 1 and Route 9 are now a major highway covered in asphalt.

The building that I would be staying in for the next two days is that of the Hotel Morin in Hue. This was the university during the war and the very building the Marines secured. I stood on the street corner, looking around and pictures of the battle that took place on this very corner began to replay in my mind.

The city of Hue was one of the fiercest battles of the Vietnam War. This is where approximately 2,500 Marines defeated 10,000 entrenched enemy troops. It was during the Vietnamese New Year holiday called Tet, the Viet Cong and the North Vietnamese Army launched a massive assault on South Vietnam. It started on January 31, 1968 and continued until February 26, 1968; a four-week battle that took the lives of 142 American service members.

It was here that Marines of the First and Fifth Regiments, supported by the U.S. Army 7th and 12th Cavalry Regiments, fought alongside the Army of the Republic of Vietnam's first Division. The Viet Cong had seized the city of Hue and approximately 138,000 citizens. After securing major buildings, including the hospital, university (now the Hotel Morin), Provincial Headquarters and Treasury building, the Marines secured the Citadel that is located across the river from our hotel.

From the window of my room, I could see the walls of the Citadel across the river, once the home of Emperors and, Buddhist monks. In the early nineteen sixties, one of the monks from the Citadel traveled to Saigon in protest of the South Vietnamese Government and set himself on fire. Hue was the site of many Buddhist's uprisings against the South Vietnamese government.

Buddhist Monks study a variety of beliefs in philosophy, science, history, and various contributions of theology. For most of history, they have lived by a strict guideline of ethics and peaceful coexistence with local beliefs and customs. Why then would one decide to set himself on fire in protest of a government trying to prevent a war? The only thing gained was war.

Located in the central part of Vietnam, Hue is a beautiful blend of Vietnamese culture with a French influence. The Imperial City gracefully preserves the magnificence of Vietnam's rich historical past. I could see why it was so important to preserve this city during the war; a symbol of everything the Vietnamese people admired and respected.

The further north on Route 9 we went, the more I saw the bottle of Grey Goose. The ghosts of the past were beckoning at the door in the minds of those I was traveling with, I realized. We were entering into the area where they spent their days here in Vietnam; the DMZ

Remnants of a church in Quang Tri riddled by war and bullets took me by surprise and reminded me of photographs I had seen from World War II. The men around me were more somber reflecting on their time many years ago in this area. We drove into the city only to see a school destroyed by both bullets and bombs. The men in my group were quiet and somber as they looked on in silence. As I stood reflecting on the battle, that terrorized this city, I noticed something very interesting. It was the direction of the sun. I pulled out my compass and noticed that I was facing the south and the building was in front of me. How could we have taken responsibility for destroying this school, when the direction of the firepower was not from the south? The holes made in this building came from the north, so why did we pay for replacement of the Quang Tri School when we did not destroy it?

In Dong Ha, large and small indentations in the landscape were still visible, with some growth in some places. Farmlands that once blanketed its fields are now covered with young rubber tree plants; a part of the revitalizing plan. Patches of vacant landscape is visible, the remnants of where dioxin was dropped. Revitalizing the area means removing mounds of soil that need to be burned in order to rid the area of the deadly poison.

Along the road, we stopped in an area where one Marine once served to pay tribute to those in his unit who never made it home. Tears filled his eyes for the first time as he remembered his days in this area and the fighting that took the life of his best friend.

We walked along a path up a small hill when I heard the whistling of the wind through the elephant grass for the first time. My heart skipped a few beats as I thought of those who had walked along this same path many years ago, wondering if the enemy was hiding behind the plush green leaves of this tall grass. The red soil, wet beneath my boots, made walking difficult at times. The path opened to a small hill and an old bunker that looked out over the valley. Its gray concrete walls sent a chill down my spine, as I felt its cold surface and felt along the small holes created by enemy fire. My skin became cold in the damp musty confines. I had a feeling of such horror come over me that I froze for a few moments. Someone asked if I was ok and I nodded my head yes. When we got outside, he said I was a combination of white and gray all at the same time.

Although I was an observer, capturing the spirit of the brave warriors of a war long ago, I was also here for a very personal reason.

Throughout my journey in Iraq, I continually thought of my brother Jack. I tried to imagine what it was like for him during Vietnam, but I could not.

I was very young when Jack joined the Marine Corps. I still remember the day when he and his friend Bobby, announced they had enlisted. That look on my father's face has stayed with me to this day. At first, I thought it was because Jack joined the Corps, when Dad was a career Army officer. As I got older, I understood what that look was. He was worried his son would be sent to war. At the time, I truly did not understand why. I only remembered my Mother crying many nights as she made dinner while my father was on the phone with someone discussing military affairs.

Jack was lucky to have come home safe, but reality hit hard when my father received a call that changed my life forever. His friend's son would never be coming home from Vietnam. This was my first experience with losing someone I knew during war. That is when I realized what war was all about. I have never forgotten that experience. Nor have I ever forgotten Ray Inslee, his smile, or that sparkle in his beautiful eyes. [Sgt Ray Inslee, U.S. Army, was killed in the Binh Dinh Province of Vietnam on March 29, 1970.] Unfortunately, I was not able to visit the place we lost Ray, but I knew in my heart he was with me in spirit while I was in country. One day I know I will find someone who served with him, then come back to this country and visit that place, but until then I had one mission to accomplish.

While traveling around a once war torn country - enjoying the beauty of its landscape, luscious delicacies, shopping, arts and culture - I visited places which were once battlegrounds for many of those in the group. One place touched my heart in a way I never expected. The one place, that for some reason meant the most to me, was Khe Sanh. It was here that my brother Jack served during the war. This, out of all others, had a direct impact on who I am today. This place caused me to miss getting to know my brother while growing up.

I stood on what they say was the old airfield and looked out over the landscape trying to imagine what it was like back when Jack was here. I nervously retrieved the cell phone from my pocket and stared at his phone number. I had never asked him any questions about his time here and was worried I would some how disturb his memories by being here. I nervously began to dial his number and as I heard the ringing in my ear, I still did not know how he would react to my calling him from this place. If there was one person who personifies Jack's demeanor concisely, it is that of the character Steven Segal plays in many of his movies; cool, calm, collected, non-reactive, non-excitable, but a man with a heart of gold.

Once I told him where I was, his response was "No Shit!" "What time is it there?" he asked. "Eight thirty in the morning," I responded. "The sun should be over your right shoulder then and you are looking at a mountain far off in the distance – that's Laos." He then began describing what I was seeing for the first time. All the while, I listened to his voice in my ear; I wished he were standing next to me. Tears began to fall. I yearned to have him with me, so I could wrap my arms around him, and tell him how much I love him. How much I cherish him for coming home to me and being such a special part of my life all these years. As the tears fell, my heart began to break because I never said the words to him that I had said to so many Vietnam Veterans before – "Welcome Home!" The pain and guilt I felt in that moment stayed with me for the rest of the trip.

I was not able to climb the hill known as Hill 881 South because edema had taken hold of my left ankle, but many of the group took the journey back up that hill. Meanwhile, those of us who could not make the trip, ventured into the village at the base of the hill. These villagers safeguarded many Americans during the war, but only two older inhabitants ventured out.

The village seemed archaic with huts made of straw and sticks standing on stilts. The villagers were warm and friendly as we began walking towards them, excited yet scared. The poverty level in the country, especially in the mountainous areas is below what we know as poverty. Yet they seem quiet content and happy to live there.

Their life is in stark contrast to the luxuries we have in America, but they were smiling so brightly. Then I thought back to the Iraqi people I had just been with. They too lived with very little and had smiles on their faces even with the little they had of possessions. I made a mental note of this observation.

Our travels took us further north to Hanoi and I must say that once we arrived in the city, the hair on my neck stood up straight. I did not feel comfortable in this city as I had in other cities we visited. I didn't feel as adventurous as I had on previous days. While everyone visited Ho Chi Minh's tomb, I stayed on the bus with one of the wives. However, I did join the group when they visited the Hanoi Hilton.

The Hoa Loa Prison, known to American prisoners of war as the Hanoi Hilton, was the prison compound used by the North Vietnamese Government to house prisoners. Conditions in this prison were miserable for those who were there. This was one of many locations used by the North Vietnamese Army to torture and interrogate American captured service members, many of whom were American pilots conducting bombing raids over the city who were shot down.

As I read how our prisoners were respected, and treated with decency, I began to get sick to my stomach. This was blatant propaganda created by the government to cover up their actions of inhuman atrocities; torture, murder and beatings, which resulted in broken bones, teeth and eardrums or dislocated limbs, and starvation because the food was contaminated with human and animal feces, not to mention the neglect of medical attention for infections and tropical diseases.

My heart sank as I peered into the rooms our pilots once lived in and I did not want to imagine the horror these men went through. I needed some air, walked out into the courtyard, and found myself standing in the very place they once stood. I remembered a picture I had copied at the Archives of them playing football or basketball and I cringed. I looked along the stone wall surrounding the courtyard and noticed the chards of glass in the mortar atop the wall. I also noticed something else, a building towering over the compound – a Hilton Hotel. I could not believe my eyes. An American based hotel chain had built a hotel right next door. I vowed in that moment to never stay at another Hilton Hotel for as long as I live.

Even though our society today will prosecute war criminals for the same crimes inflicted on military personnel and civilians alike, our own country never charged North Vietnam for violating the Geneva Convention. One has to wonder why they would have allowed this type of behavior to go unpunished. Maybe if they had made this information known, things might have been different. Instead, our elected officials in Washington hid behind calling this was a police action allowing the torture and dishonor of American Service Members, because without declaring it a war the Geneva Convention was never applied.

To this day, the Vietnamese government claims that those who were held in the Hanoi Hilton were imprisoned as criminals, "pirates" and "bandits" who had attacked Vietnam without authority, and were not POWs. Did they not realize there was a war going on?

While traveling throughout the country I saw not only its beauty, but also remnants of the war fought more than forty years ago. Thoughts of both Jack and Ray came to mind repeatedly, but so did the memories of those I was with in Iraq. I thought of the Marines I was with only a few months ago and wondered how they were getting along. Almost every day I felt the slight twinge of guilt take hold of me for enjoying myself.

When I returned home from this trip and my mind began to clear from the jet lag, the thoughts, feelings and magnitude of these two trips combined brought me to my knees with such pain and guilt.

For the next six months I plunged myself into my work and my objectives of finishing the original intent of this project. I continued with my research and conducted interviews, but had difficulty putting words to paper. The objective was to tell the story of these brave warriors I have had the honor of being associated with most of my life, but instead I found myself writing about my recent experiences with the military, their families and it turned into telling another story, a story of discovery.

My dilemma caused me to contact one of my mentors, a Vietnam Veteran. He listened to my problem and his response put everything into perspective. He pointed out a few important key elements that I had not realized until that day. "Tell your story first of why you went to Iraq and Vietnam. That story needs to be told in order to set the stage for the bigger picture. Your story now intertwines with my story as a veteran. It intertwines with the heroes who protected you in Iraq. It is a story that is long over due, because it deals with families, warriors, and the American people as a whole. Your story will tell my story in how it affected me as a veteran upon my return home. I told you before you left on your journey that it was going to change you forever and it did. You have had the unique privilege and honor to live and walk in my boots for a short time, you now understand a little of what I feel and that is rare for a civilian to understand. Others who have gone to war as media will never understand what we go through because they only want the political story. They are detached from us, your not – you're part of our family. You also lived the experience differently than they ever would have, because you were willing to do that, the Marines you were with gave you a unique gift –

they allowed you to feel that trust only those in combat ever feel. Through your story, you will be able to tell my story. You went into a combat zone with your eyes open wider than any other media would have done – because the passion for our military is in your heart and soul. That's what is missing in their stories." When he was done speaking, I was in tears far more than I ever thought possible. No veteran had ever spoken to me like that before. I was humbled.

I thought about what he said and how my life had intertwined with so many veterans over the years. As a result, I could not sleep because I had so much weighing heavily on my mind. When I awoke the next morning, it dawned on me that this whole experience might have been for a different purpose than I had originally planned it to be. I now felt an obligation to tell a story of the legacy we are all a part of - it is not about any one single American who goes into a combat zone - it is about everyone associated with those who put on the uniform. This includes the public, and how they perceive our military, not to mention politicians, media and Hollywood who never seem to see the bigger picture. Although my story intertwines with theirs, it is their story nonetheless.

CHAPTER 27
FAMILIES
THE UNSUNG HEROES

When a warrior is sent into combat, their family enters into a different type of combat zone; a life struggling to contain their emotions.

There is not a day that goes by that they do not worry about their warrior. Their emotions are raw during this period and they find themselves getting emotional while making dinner, taking out the garbage, or just going to the store for milk.

For the rest of us, it is just another day. Without the warrior being a part of the family unit, they struggle to maintain every day existence. The constant worry, stress and juggling can weigh on a spouse. Some seek out comfort from others whose spouse has been deployed, while others go down a different path altogether.

As the wife of a career Army Officer, my Mother always said it takes a very special person to be married to someone in the military. She used to say that to be married to a warrior; a spouse must be independent, self-disciplined and capable of being alone during long periods of separation. They must be father and mother, repairperson, chauffer, disciplinarian, all the while holding it together emotionally at the same time. To other spouses they must be the ultimate representative of their spouse, because everything they do reflects back on the future of their warrior while in uniform. They must also know and understand that they are not number one in their spouses life – the military is. This is why I have always said the spouse of a warrior is more than just an unsung hero; they are the lifeblood of our armed forces.

During my time in country, many of my conversations with warriors turned to loved ones back home. They talked about their having to juggle everything while they were away; kids, homework, the house, medical benefits, college, family members, and maintenance of a car. There were also talks about plans for the future and mistakes of the past.

Everyday as we went out on patrols, I wondered about those they left behind. Just before the vehicle would pass the gate, I would see the sign "Complacency kills – Be Alert" and I would quietly say a prayer for the safety of the warriors around me, and their families back home. During those moments, I tried to picture a wife or girlfriend back home, wondering all the while, what they were doing to occupy their days. Wondering how the kids were holding up and what they did to keep them occupied.

While the adrenaline flows through their veins, scanning the road and surrounding terrain for possible danger, they clear their mind of everything except the mission at hand.

Meanwhile back home, those left behind struggle to maintain their sanity and keep the home fires burning. They put a smile on their face as if nothing could bother them. They tell themselves this is just another deployment, nothing to worry about as they count down the days until their warrior comes home and plan that special welcome home celebration. While they gather up supplies and prepare that special care package, there is a knock at the door. They freeze in their steps, their heart begins to race and a chill of pure panic runs down their spine; terror takes hold of their thoughts. It is probably just an innocent deliveryman, a neighbor or the mail carrier. To an average person, this would be nothing, but to a family member it could mean something altogether different. Without looking out the window to ease their mind, they think the worst and wonder if there are uniforms on the other side of the door about to tell them their world has just been turned upside down.

Military life is not for those who are the weak of heart. While playing both parents and taking care of their own family, they help others in need within the military community. They are the shoulder to cry upon when another is sick, or having a bad day. They are the extended arms who render that much needed hug when one is feeling overwhelmed and needs strength. When they feel their walls crashing down around them, the strength of each other reminds them to pull up their boot strings, or big girl panties and carry on as best they can. To each other, they are the sounding board when things go wrong, encouraging each other to be strong. They turn to each other so they can be there for their warrior.

Those that have been in a military family know that there may come a time (although they pray it will never happen) when the knock on the door is not a neighbor or delivery person. This is when the spouse of a military person turns to another in the military family for comfort. A spouse or parent is never prepared for that knock. No matter what the military rank is, a spouse needs another spouse or parent to comfort him or her. In those first few hours, it is just as devastating to those giving comfort to feel the loss of losing a sister or brother.

When that knock occurs, those within the military community surround each other. As the walls come crashing down around them, it is the extended families that help in those first few hours. Sitting with them, holding them, comforting them and helping their birth family understand how to cope with them. After the initial shock is over, they are there to help pick up the pieces of their lives while still maintaining their own family and home.

All the while knowing this could have been them, should there be a knock at their door. The spouse of a warrior helps to make phone calls, send out emails or run errands. Even though you are the outsider in that family, they become the voice for a fallen warrior and their family. They fight for the rights of their spouse and family. They say it is as if once a warrior is killed in combat, their country looks past their spouse as if the spouse is just another casualty of war.

They watch as their friend changed from the hated word of "dependent" to new status of Un Re-Wed Widow (URW). They are transformed from once being an active part of the military community to a member of an elite group of men and women who have lost one of their own. It is an unnerving situation to be in when a spouse understands the reality of their loss; no matter how many seconds, minutes, hours, days or weeks that they spend trying to help them begin to pick up the pieces, they cannot bring home what they have lost.

Their worrying began the day they said good-bye to their warrior as they got on that bus, headed for a combat zone. They were either emotionless or overly emotional on that drive home. Too many conversations that were never had, many things left unsaid, not enough "I love you" whispered.

As they look around their community, watch the news, or read the paper, they wonder what is going through peoples' minds. To the protesters, who say we should not be in a war, or to those who say we should not be there at all, they want to scream and say, "Go home and hug their family and be thankful they have them." For those that protest the war, they pray they will never know what it feels like to have lost a person they love to combat. They will never know or understand never being able to share their hopes, dreams, fears, or undying love with ever again.

On the refrigerator of one Army spouse, hangs a magnet that looks like a want ad in a newspaper, which says, "Army wife wanted, Sissies need not apply." Although this is for the Army, I believe it fits the criteria of all those who marry military personnel. I also believe that it is what my mother made me understand as a child. It depicts one that stands strong, takes time to learn what they can about the military life and its regulations, and who makes the military work for them and their family, not the other way around.

CHAPTER 28
HOME FRONT – HISTORY REPEATING ITSELF

It started in the sixties when students revolted against the establishment on every level, and gathered to protest at the drop of a dime. They did not need a reason, nor did they want to understand why they were protesting, they were happy to be a part of something.

In March of 1966, President Johnson announced he would be sending more troops to Vietnam, thus escalating the war. Vietnam was a fight entered into to help the South Vietnamese government and its people defend their freedom against North Vietnamese guerilla insurgents terrorizing citizens for control of their country. American students who did not understand international politics, the South East Asia Treaty Agreement signed after World War II, or our pledge to help defend smaller countries that could not defend themselves, or what could be lost here at home as a result, gathered to protest against something they knew nothing about.

Fearful of having to pick up a rifle, they took to the streets protesting the war. Many were pacifists, dissenters, or drug addicts resisting the draft. The majority were the children of those of privilege, who were afraid to defend the very country that gave them the riches they enjoyed daily. Among them were former service members who returned home from war disgruntled and claimed it was an illegal rule of authority.

As time passed the war heated up, and those who were searching to score acid, pot, pills and other drugs joined in protest. Mothers who were grieving the loss of their sons wanted someone to blame and thus joined the protest against the war, further dishonoring their memory. They carried flag-draped boxes, which represented those who had given the ultimate sacrifice. Protestors became extremely confrontational and anarchy began. This was the beginning of America dividing.

While we find ourselves facing a changing time in the present, we have not learned the lessons of the past; history is beginning to repeat itself once again. In today's environment, the individuals formerly Vietnam Protesters have now become educators fueling the fires of the past, they now teach ignorance. They are gathering once again to revolt against something they do not understand – terrorism.

Just as it was during the Vietnam War, there are American Soldiers, Sailors, Airman and Marines being disrespected when returning home from a combat zone. They are beginning spat upon and beaten by fellow Americans. Many do not want to wear their uniforms on trains or while traveling. Families in mourning during funerals for a fallen warrior are disrupted by protesters more interested in their own political statements. College officials with no leadership skills allow students to disrespect pro-American speakers. This further helps erode support of our armed forces and disrespects their sacrifices in a combat zone.

As it was in the past, the above problems are once again plaguing our country as our service members come home from Iraq and Afghanistan. They are facing the same problems their fathers and brothers once faced, but this time the stakes are even higher than they were before. Terrorism is festering within our communities and is an enemy that cannot be seen with the naked eye. We will not feel their blow until they have fostered enough complacency among the people and then they will strike. Their strike will be far greater than it ever was on September 11, 2001, unless we as a country open our eyes and see what is happening around us.

In today's society, protesters lay blame at the feet of our military rather than take responsibility for the seeds of dissension they sow. This type of mentality makes the military feel as though they are a closed society, alone in the fight against terrorism.

While the government fails in their efforts to explain the good that is being accomplished, no one is asking service members how they feel about fighting and the purpose for which they are fighting. No one has asked a service member what differences he or she has made thus far. Why is it that our service members are doing all the explaining of finding caches of weapons, disarming the insurgents, or the goodwill that is accomplished? Why is it that the government is not saying these things, or better yet, our media and politicians? Why is it the service member who is the only one educating their fellow Americans on the good that is being accomplished?

The media measures the war based on the number of casualties and using their tag line of "If it bleeds it leads." Just as in the past, no one is controlling media's propaganda campaign for political reasons. "Sick" service members are being touted as the norm, while "normal" service members are simply drinking the Pentagon's Kool-Aid. Politicians call service members Nazi's and Terrorists. Then we have the most destructive of all, people who know nothing about duty, honor or sacrifice, defacing War Memorials, further demoralizing our country and it has fallen.

In January of 2007 a group of protestors, mirroring the past, gathered in Washington, DC to protest the war in Iraq. They gathered for the pretence of making their voices heard before Congress, but they made one major mistake – they defaced the steps of the Capitol with their anti-war messages. Those that carried out these criminal acts did so with malice and were not interested in freedom of speech, lawful assembly, or the liberties this country affords them. Their actions were strictly for personal gain. Like an enemy of war, they too manipulated the media to achieve their fifteen minutes of fame and bring attention to their cause. This type of destruction of public property is a crime, yet nothing is done to prevent it. Freedom of speech and expression is a privilege, not a license to destroy.

It happened again on March 17, 2007, and in September of 2007 when these same groups returned to our Nation's Capitol for a march on the Pentagon and protest against the war. They gathered at veteran's memorials, the Pentagon and the White House for their anti-war speeches. Their plans to deface all veterans' memorials along the Mall were thwarted by people they never thought would gather – Vietnam Veterans standing shoulder to shoulder with Veterans of Iraq and Afghanistan.

"Political Correctness" (which has a communist origin) is to control the thoughts of those they wish to control.

At a time when our country should be uniting our energies in support of those who are fighting to root out terrorism, we are fueling the fires of terrorist activities on the streets of Iraq and Afghanistan. We are also directing this energy against each other, instead of the enemy at hand.

History is repeating itself right under our nose and it is time we stand together against those who do not understand the perils of the enemy. If we lose the fight against terrorism, we will lose our country. We will lose our virtues and values; we will lose our inner strength. We will lose the foundation on which this country was created, freedom. Our enemies are capitalizing on own ignorance.

CHAPTER 29
JOURNEY BEGINS TO COME FULL CIRCLE
AT A WELCOME HOME

Every writer dreams of one single experience in which to write from, but never seem to find it for one reason or another. Call it destiny or fate, which blessed me with such a special experience that has been an emotional roller coaster. A roller coaster that is still speeding down the tracks, twisting and turning every day, filled with a sense of excitement, fear, joy, laughter, struggle, and yes, even sorrow. A fate that has twisted many times, but never revealing what the ending will be. However, it has revealed one thing thus far, enlightenment into a side of our military I was deficient in – combat life experience. Many asked if I would be willing to do it all over again and without hesitation, I have to say, in a heartbeat. After all, life is a journey to experience fully. If I had allowed any fear to stand in the way of the journey, I would have missed something very special.

I have had one golden rule while dealing with the military; keep my personal feelings separate from my working relationships. This journey forced me to truly get close; down and dirty with the Marines I traveled with. Because of this closeness, when it was time to close that chapter of my journey with this unit, I found it extremely difficult to turn the last page for many reasons.

Like any other writer, I started out looking for the stories, which would tell of the bravery, heroism and sacrifice. What I found was something entirely different in the end.

The Marines of the Third Land Assault Reconnaissance Battalion transformed me. They found a way to penetrate the solid walls around my heart, and humbled me at the same time. They challenged me beyond my own comprehension of understanding while teaching me about their life in a combat zone. It was for this reason alone that I honored them upon their return home in person.

The Welcome Home

The day was September 29, 2006. It was a beautiful California day, with its clear blue skies. The warm desert breeze touched my cheek as I stepped off the plane in Palm Springs. Although exhausted from traveling, I was returning to a desert oasis for a special mission. In a few hours, my special protectors of the United States Marine Corps' 3rd LAR Battalion would be stepping off a plane and touching U.S. Soil for the first time in many months. I was invigorated.

I had the opportunity to meet some of the wives of that special unit after I checked into my hotel. We talked about their struggles and fears during the deployment. While I listened to the wives tell me their stories, I began flashing back to my time in Iraq. I recalled many conversations and quietly in my head, I could hear the many expressions of love and admiration for wives, family and children back home.

It was strange because I knew their husbands in a completely different way. They were not just Marines to me, these men were my heroes; and they allowed me the honor to enter their sacred world of military life in a combat zone. While I listen to their voices, I tried to understand their sacrifices, but something happened to me instead. Instead of trying to find the right words to express their thoughts and feelings, I began feeling their raw emotions within me.

I began to wonder how I could I express my gratitude to these wonderful women for what their husbands had done for me. How does one tell a wife that their husband taught me so much about living and surviving in a combat zone? I do not think I will ever be able to express my gratitude to them, or to their Marines.

As I got to know these women, I began to feel detached from my heroes. The women sitting before me represented all the wives and family members I had heard so much about. I began to feel as though I was intruding on their private time for being there to enjoy the welcome home celebrations, which would be happening later that night. Although I was excited right along with them, I began to feel as though I was an outsider; they were not my husband, son or brother, only my heroes.

Later that evening it was time for the welcome home activities at Victory Field. I have been to many a deployment farewells and welcome home parties in the past, but this one was so much more special to me. These warriors earned a very special place in my heart.

It was great to meet the other family members: the other wives, sisters, brothers, parents and even the children. While we all waited for the news that those Marines were back on base we laughed, joked and told stories of these special warriors. All the while, my emotions began to build, but still I felt out of place among the families. No matter how much the Marines and family members let me in, I was still an outsider and I was becoming accustomed to that position.

The announcement came over the loud speakers and said the words we longed to hear "The Marines have arrived and are at the Armory," I sneaked off to welcome them home in private.

I approached the armory, and there they were - tired and weary - standing in line waiting to secure their weapons. Those same emotions that crept up on me the night before I left Iraq began to surface once again. I wanted to yell Welcome Home so badly, but the words would not come out. I quietly walked among the Marines standing in line and could hear whispers: "Who is that?" Then all of a sudden, a sense of surprise came from one muffled voice, "I think that's Betty, he said. I turned, looked in the direction of the voice, smiled brightly and nodded as tears began to fill my eyes. My lips moved, but no words came out.

One by one, they began to gather by the concrete wall behind the armory. They would wait for orders to board the buses that would bring them to Victory field. As I looked up and down the wall, my heart felt as though it would jump out of my chest. My heroes were finally home.

I knew how tired and weary they felt after two days of traveling to get this far. Although before I left Iraq, I had joked about collecting my hugs and kisses from every one of them upon their return, now it did not seem right to collect them before their wives, girlfriends, parents and children had that honor.

Those beautiful weary smiles were better than any hug or kiss I was promised. My heroes of 3LAR BN were home, that was enough for me.

The Ride To Victory Field

While the Marines finished receiving their briefing, I had the opportunity to meet some very special men and women who escorted them back to base that evening on motorcycles. They were members of the Patriot Guard.

Although I had never had the privilege of meeting any of their members before, I had heard rumors about the Patriot Guards for their selfless acts of escorting and protecting the families at funerals of our fallen warriors. However, I did not know they also provided escort service to units coming home.

What an amazing opportunity this was to witness. I learned they are from many walks of life; Vietnam Veterans, Veterans of the Gulf War, Operation Enduring Freedom, Operation Iraqi Freedom, and Patriotic Americans who support our military. These wonderful angels took time out of their day to perform this wonderful tribute to our warriors and I had to personally thank them for what they did for my favorite Marines.

During one of our conversations, one of the guards, a Marine who was part of the unit coming home that night, told them who I was and why I was there. We laughed and joked about my time in Iraq and subsequent trip to Vietnam. After I expressed a few tales of my journey, Ed, a Vietnam Veteran and one of the Guards, asked if I had a problem with riding on the back of a motorcycle. I laughed and said, "If given a chance, that's my favorite form of transportation." He smiled and gave me a very special gift. "How would you like to help us escort these Marines back to their family by riding on the back of my bike?" I looked around at the others, smiling and nodding their heads in agreement, I was lost for words, but accepted the invitation gladly, as I fought back the tears with such a special honor.

We began rolling down the road toward Victory field, I could hear the engines of the buses behind us, and my heart was bursting with joy. We turned the corner and the field came into view. It looked like a football field, with its floodlights and plush green grass. That night the field was clear; there was no game, but there was a crowd for something, something very special.

The bikes began to get closer and my excitement began to build as the roar of the crowd got louder and louder, then it happened – that feeling of coming home took hold of me. The louder the crowds screamed, the more my emotions began to let go and the tears began to fall hard. Instead of feeling the guilt of leaving them behind in Iraq, it was being replaced with pure relief. Although I was not the driver of that bike, that short ride gave me a feeling of helping to bring my heroes back to their loved ones. What an amazing feeling it was to feel that sense of relief and closure.

This was one of those experiences every writer dreams of. Because on that ride I was not just a writer, but an American helping to escort those Marines home.

Thank you Ed, Candyman and your fellow Patriot Guards for giving me such a wonderful gift. Little did you know you were giving me the closure I needed to say farewell to my heroes.

Another Side of These Warriors.

On Sunday morning, I sat drinking a cup of coffee gathering my thoughts, outside the restaurant of the hotel, and was surprised to see one of the Marines walking towards me. He came to have brunch with his wife and children. I watched as he sat along side the pool, his feet dangling in the water, playing with his son, dipping those tiny little feet in and out of the water, laughing the whole time. I remembered how much he said he had missed his kids and his wife, he loved them dearly.

To see him as dad and husband was a beautiful sight to see. It made waking up early that morning that much more special.

Many of the Marines found out where I was staying and throughout the day, they ventured over for coffee, or to just say hello with wives, girlfriends and children in tow. This was a very special surprise since I had not expected to see them so soon. We laughed, joked and reminisced about our time in country. It was nice to finally be able to put a face with a story as I met family members.

Later that evening, I sat alone eating dinner and noticed a few of the Marines with wives, or girlfriends, enjoying a romantic dinner in the outdoor café. They sat under a full moon listening to soft romantic music at one of the café styled tables, covered by a soft linen tablecloth, as candles flickered off the crystal blue water of the pool. Those special lovebirds sat quietly, not saying a word to one another, just gazing into each other's eyes, holding hands occasionally. I could tell their bodies where there, but their minds had not caught up with them yet. They had a look about their face as if to say, "Is this for real or is this another one of those damn dreams." These were moments they dreamed about so many nights laying in their cots. The little smiles, soft stares and that special wink told what was in their hearts.

Even thought they knew I was not far away, I stayed away giving them their privacy. As reality set in and they rekindled the spark that has been dormant within their souls, I began to see that warm glow capture their hearts once again. I could not help but smile. Being the romantic that I am, it warmed my heart to see them this way.

Many of these men shared long conversations with me while in the desert. I recalled many of those conversations as I gazed upon them now sitting across from that special woman who owned their heart. Just seeing them like this gave me a different side of these strong warriors that I once knew.

I began the final stages of my closure with this unit, I was happy to see them interacting with family and loved ones. No matter where I go or what I do in life, these Marines will always hold a special place in my heart and I will always be protective over these men. It's easier to begin my closure now because I know they are in very good hands with people and family that love them just as much as I do and even more. Unfortunately, there is one final detail that needs to be secured before I can close this part of this wonderful journey, a detail that is going to be hard to accomplish for sure.

CHAPTER 30
EIGHT FALLEN BROTHERS

A light drizzle began to fall as I stepped out of the car in front of the ceremonial field. I looked up to the heavens and wondered if this was a sign of the kind of day I had in front of me. I walked slowly to the field trying to contain my emotions. The row of rifles standing at attention with helmets on top came into view and I stopped, frozen, fighting back the tears. I had been to memorial services in the past, but not like this one. This would be the first in which I personally was in the combat zone with those who these rifles represented, in this case five.

A young Marine motioned for me to take a seat in an area designated for VIP Guests, but I ignored him and continued walking towards the grass below. I needed to say a private good-bye before anyone else showed up.

As I walked along the row of rifles, I reached out and touched each helmet. With each touch, I felt the pain of a knife thrusting into my heart as I thought of each of these warriors. Feelings of guilt began to take hold of me, one question hit me –why did I come home alive, and they had not? I had already lived my life and they were so young.

I walked back to the reviewing stand and happened upon a few of those I had not seen at the homecoming. We exchanged solemn smiles and I received shocked comments that I had ventured out so far from home for this special event. Yet, they knew the reason why I was there; it was evident in my eyes.

As in every war throughout history there has always been a price paid, the ultimate sacrifice of a fallen comrade. That day was unlike any other day for me because I could remember the laughter, the voices, their sensitivity, a talented voice, and their mutual love of being a Marine. I began to remember a few discussions of family, kids and that bright future. I was brought back to the present when the Battalion arrived and took their place. I elected to stand alone along side of the seating area with the other media. I could not sit.

The military have many rituals, which they perform on a daily basis, but a memorial service to a fallen brother is unlike any other detail; it is taken much more seriously. A memorial service for a fallen brother is one of the hardest duties any Soldier, Sailor, Airman, Marine or Coast Guardsman has to perform. Although hard, they find the strength to endure because it honors those who gave the ultimate sacrifice in the protection of Country, Freedom and most of all their brothers in arms.

It is always hard to hear of the passing of a brother. When one hears the news of a fallen hero, your mind freezes and refuses to accept the news just given to you. Your first thoughts are disbelief because you always thought that person was, or seemed invincible. Then reality kicks in and a face comes into our memories.

As I stood in the damp grass, I briefly turned the pages of the memorial booklet I was handed. I looked at the faces and I began to smile. Baucus of Montana told me about his beautiful bride of only seven short months. I joked with him about being a Baucus and from Montana, asking if he was related to Senator Max Baucus and sure enough, he laughed, "Yup, sure am he's my Uncle." I thought about Hanson and his beautiful voice. Butterfield with his great sense of humor, standing over me like a father, telling me how to keep my body armor closed so I could get home and make him and all the rest famous; Williams and his love of anything fast, Galvez and his great sense of humor and smile. Then the ceremony began.

Although I was listening to the Marines speaking of their feelings for their friends, my emotions began to take hold of me. I began to tremble, and the tears began to flow as if a faucet was turned on. Gunnery Sergeant Cox of the Public Affairs Office walked by and noticed I was breaking down. Without saying a word, he placed his hand on my shoulder in an effort to console me. Little did he know that one gesture gave me the strength to endure the rest of the ceremony.

I was not the only one who broke down. I heard a faint moan and as I looked over at the formation, two Marines were escorting another from the line who had been overcome with grief.

Even though I am Irish and I love the sounds of a well-played bagpipe, that day I could not listen to one for any amount of money in the world. I tried to think of other things, so I did not have to hear the music. I knew if I allowed my ears to hear the pipes, I was done for. I silently walked away from the area in which I was standing in order to compose myself once again.

When the ceremony was finished, I left the base for the last time. I drove out the gate and was filled with sadness at the loss of my affiliation with this very special group of Marines. When I returned to the hotel, I headed straight for the bar and ordered a shot of tequila. I sat with the shot in hand, said a little pray and toasted it up to those of the 3 LAR Battalion. I downed the shot and went back to my room to pack my suitcase. It was time to go home and finally close this chapter of my journey.

CHAPTER 31
A GHOST IS PUT TO REST

During my journey throughout Vietnam, I experienced many things, but one thing gnawed at me, the name Bobby kept creeping into my mind. Something was telling me I needed to call Bobby, but I couldn't figure out who Bobby was.

It was not until Labor Day weekend when I placed a call to Ray's Mom to tell her about my experience of going to Vietnam that I found out who Bobby was. After I told her that I could feel Ray with me throughout the trip, I also mentioned the strange notion of needing to call someone named Bobby.

She laughed at me and said call him. "Call who, I said," I was puzzled not knowing who she was talking about. Now you have to understand when I think of Ray's little brother, I think of Robert. I had never called him Bobby, or at least I never remember calling him that. Once she said it, I laughed at my own stupidity. Of course, that must be who I am to call. His mom gave me the number and I said I would call him the following evening.

Later that night I took a ride to the Vietnam Memorial to visit Panel 12W in the hopes that I might find the words to open my conversation with Bobby.

The Vietnam War Memorial located in Washington, DC is a place where many can shed the ghosts from the past. A peaceful place where the warriors, their family and friends come to heal the wounds left behind.

To each of those who visit the Wall, their ghosts have a different meaning. Some may be dealing with words never spoken, dreams unfilled, but for many they are the horrors associated with combat and the loss of a friend.

I visit the hallowed grounds of the Wall as often as I can. I have never forgotten them or the sacrifice they gave. When I walk along the path, I say a silent prayer for the names etched on each panel, but I only stop at one panel; that panel is 12W. Standing before this special panel, I touch my fingers to my lips, and then reach above my head to line 57 to the name of the one person I knew personally, Raymond Inslee. Ray served proudly with the 173rd Airborne Brigade, A Company, 1st Battalion, 503rd Infantry Regiment during his time in country.

Throughout the years, each time I have left those hallowed grounds I vowed to one day find someone who served with him, who could tell me about the man who touched my life so many years ago. When I embarked on this journey, I never dreamed of finding anyone who could help me fulfill the vow I made before Panel 12W so many times.

I made my call to Bobby the following night and learned that he followed in both our father's and Ray's footsteps by joining the Army, serving with the 82nd Airborne. Ray would have been so proud of him.

He described his passion for helping to preserve the memory of his brother, and all others who gave the ultimate sacrifice in Vietnam. This I had to agree was a worthy cause.

After catching up on the years that got away from us, he mentioned he had come across a website for the 173$^{RD.}$ It was ironic that during the time I was in Iraq, Bobby posted his message on the website asking if anyone who served with A Company, 1st BN, 503rd of the 173rd Airborne Brigade knew his brother. Two months later, while I was in Vietnam, he received a response from a man who said he not only knew him, but also served with him in Vietnam. Talk about a divine intervention.

I was so excited to hear the news I began asking all sorts of questions. Is he willing to talk to you? Have you spoken to him? What is he like? Bobby said he was not ready to talk to him yet. My heart skipped a beat as I gathered the courage to ask if I could. He gladly gave me the information so I could contact him directly.

I was emotional beyond words after receiving this information and found it hard to find the words to write to a man I have never met before and ask permission to speak to him. Normally it would be a piece of cake for me to draft up such a letter, but this was different; it was personal. I was not sure if he would be willing to speak to me; much less talk about a fallen brother after all these years. I looked at Ray's picture, which hangs on my wall above my desk, and asked him to help guide me in finding the right words of inspiration and strength that would invoke this man to agree to speak to me.

Once I began to write, I wrote from the heart and it did not take long for the words to appear on paper. After hitting the send button my email was off into cyber space, on its way to Larry Hampton. I nervously waited for a response. I imagined it would take a few days before I heard a word. I tried not to think about it the rest of the evening and went to sleep.

A little after midnight, something woke me up and I sat straight up trying to figure out what it was. Something was telling me to check my email. Still half asleep, I stumbled to my computer and brought up the mailbox. I tried to focus my eyes and there on the screen was one message waiting for me; a response from Larry Hampton. At first, I thought I was dreaming until I read his message. Even though I was still semi asleep, I woke up quickly as my heart began to beat faster.

Larry was as excited as I was to have found someone who knew Ray. His message granted me my wish to speak to him on the phone about his time in country with Ray. I was on cloud nine after I read his message and looked up at Ray's picture as tears welled up in my eyes.

There were many conversations between Larry and me over the course of the next few weeks. He explained where they were and what they were doing during that timeframe. Although LZ Uplift was their main camp, they lived in an abandoned church just north of the base. He educated me about their unit. Then over the phone, he taught me how to read military maps, so I could pin point where they were. We continued to laugh and reminisce about Ray and our special relationship with him, the funny antics of my childhood and their time in Binh Dinh.

Three weeks later, I boarded a plane, bound for Atlanta to attend an event to help raise money for a memorial to the fallen of the 173rd and I meet Larry Hampton in person. The event was a celebration of life, service and brotherhood, for those who served with the 173rd. It was an evening of music provided by Big & Rich and other performers, who volunteered their time for this special fundraiser. One song that touched everyone's heart was that of "The 8th of November," a song written by Big Kenny and John Rich dedicated to those of 173rd who served in Vietnam. Hearing this song live, surrounded by veterans of Vietnam and those who just returned from Afghanistan and Iraq, the tears began to fall. Overcome by our emotions Larry and I clung to each other, as the music took hold of our hearts and the mutual loss of our beloved Ray.

Larry having been the point man for Ray's unit, like so many other Vietnam Veterans, grief and guilt of a fallen brother takes a toll on ones heart. Having left the unit the day before that fateful day, Larry was like many of his brothers in grieving the loss of Ray.

Our conversations during the previous weeks were like a set of keys, each key opened the vault to another piece of the puzzle. The one key that would help me put the final pieces of the puzzle together I received over breakfast the next morning.

Larry and I met for breakfast in the hotel restaurant and talked privately. He began to relay the story of 29 March 1970 and I listened intently.

Staring down at hands crossed in his lap, he began, "I was back at LZ Uplift awaiting orders to leave for a specialized school when I got the news that my unit was hit." Larry said in a solemn voice. "As soon as I got the news, I left the base and quickly headed north towards the church. I wasn't concerned about getting into trouble, these were my men and I didn't care."

"Ray was special you know. Everyone liked him. No matter what he took on, he did it with gusto. He wanted to learn everything he could from the first day he joined us. He was a good soldier, a good leader, and a good friend." His thoughts drifting off as he looked out over the parking lot. "I was point man until I left the day before, then he took over my position," he said softly as tears began to well up in his eyes.

"They were walking point along a trail just north of the church, at the base of the mountain ridge when it happened.

That area was known as an access point for the VC." His voice trailed off. "Ray was in front. The four of them were wounded, but by the time I got there, he was already gone," he added quietly, as the tears began to fall. I reached out and held his hand knowing how hard it was for him remembering. We sat together in silence, each knowing no more words were needed.

I gingerly asked a few more questions; received the answers I was in search of, and then the discussion was closed forever.

Throughout the following months we talked on the phone all the time and exchanged emails which further educated me on their time in country. It would not be until a cold, snowy overcast day in March 2007 that I would see Larry again face to face.

My journey would begin to come full circle when I entered the hallowed grounds of the black granite wall with someone very special. I had made a vow many times over to find someone who had served with Ray, and I had. Part of that vow was to bring that person with me on one of my visits to the wall. On this visit, I was fulfilling my promise as Larry and I visited the wall together, a journey we wanted to take together; it was personal for both of us.

We slowly walked along the path, holding on to each other not saying a word. At first, I was surprised I did not feel any emotions. Then, like a faucet, the tears began to fall as we stood in front of Panel 12W and Ray's name. As I had done on so many occasions in the past, I touched my fingers to my lips and then touched the name etched into the cold black granite. For the first time, the granite did not feel cold to my touch; it felt warm. I smiled at the thought that he knew we were there.

Silently, I began to talk to him as I have done on so many other visits. I told him how happy I was to have finally found someone else who knew him all those years ago. I thanked him for giving me the signs that helped me make that call last summer. For helping me to find Larry so I could learn that he was not alone at the end, he was with a brother who loved him just as much. As I finished my thoughts, I felt a warm sensation wrap around me, like a blanket of peace and love and I felt Ray was with us in that moment. I would like to think that he was letting me know that he was happy that I had found Larry and we had visited him together.

In that same moment, my heart felt lighter and I began to realize I was allowing my special ghost to leave me and finally begin to rest.

The Presentation

It would not be until May of 2008 that my journey would come full circle while attending a memorial celebration at the Vietnam Memorial with motorcycle riders from all across the nation.

On Sunday morning, Major Andras Marton, United States Army and Father Mike Kifly of Pennsylvania, walked with me down the gravel stones toward Panel 12W on a special mission for Larry Hampton. Larry asked that I present a plaque at the base of the panel in honor of Ray on his behalf; a mission I was honored to perform for a friend. After Father Mike offered up a prayer for those who gave the ultimate sacrifice and all those who serve in our military, I quietly slipped a piece of paper from my pocket and placed it next to Larry's plaque.

This was the first time in all the years I had stood before this panel that I had written anything to Ray and placed it at the wall.

Presented to the Wall on May 24, 2008

To My Darling Ray, My Guardian Angel

38 Years ago you promised to return to us as just another soldier. Instead, they sent you home a Hero.

With each passing day, you remind me you are still with me, because:
With every Sunrise, I see your smile
With every crack of Thunder, I feel your strength
With every Breeze, a gentle kiss touches my cheek
With every Step I take, your heart beats another day
In every drop of Rain that falls upon my skin, I feel your warm embrace
In every howling wind, I hear your roaring laughter

In every tear I shed, another link to life is forever thread
I have never forgotten you!

CHAPTER 32
JOURNEY ENDS WITH SPECIAL GIFTS

My journey into the truth began with one road. A road that twisted many times and I found myself standing at a junction with multiple roads. Roads that overlapped personal and political agendas. I chose one road and ultimately found that it intertwined with the others, each providing subtle clues. Like a beacon in the night, each clue guided me to more than just the truth.

They taught me valuable lessons and I discovered something along the way. Like the pieces of a puzzle with thousands of different shapes, sizes and colors fitting together to show a bigger picture, I found pearls of wisdom as well as the truth.

One clear message came through on this journey from every service member– "I wish I could express, first hand, the true nature of what it means to serve this country in uniform. It is not about medals or pay; it is about what it means to be a Soldier, Sailor, Airman, Marine, or Coastguardsman who stands ready to fight for their country."

They are often relegated to; "Those who we want to have, but should not be seen," and are burned in effigy when they give of themselves only to return home to an ungrateful nation. Regardless of public and political opinion of them, these brave Americans stand ready, willing, and able to protect this country and defend its freedom.

The Marines of 3LAR and 6th Civil Affairs taught me a great deal on this journey, and without their ever knowing it, they sent me home with many gifts. Gifts I will never be able to thank them personally for giving me.

1) The gift of learning what it is like to live in their boots for a short time

2) The gift of teaching me how to survive with very little

3) The gift of adapting and overcoming my fears and adversities put before me

4) The gift of new eyes to see the world around me

5) The gift of a new understanding of the world in which we live

6) The gift to know that one can live simply and be truly happy

7) The gift of a new understanding of our Armed Forces of the United States

8) The gift of new perspective to understand what others went through during another war.

9) The gift of newfound love for freedom and liberty

10) The gift of giving back to those around us

11) The gift of trust in another human being

12) The gift of friendship, which will last a lifetime

13) The gift of shedding tears for those who have given the ultimate sacrifice for all of us.

14) The gift that freedom is not free – for there can never be value placed upon it when life, liberty and the pursuit of happiness is at stake.

The most important gift you gave me was the key to being an American. A key that is deep in the heart and soul of every member of the Army, Navy, Air Force, Marine Corps, and Coast Guard.

15) The gift of reminding me what it is to be an American.

With this new understanding, I know I have a responsibility to you and my fellow Americans' to uphold what is written in the Declaration of Independence and Constitution of the United States of America; to defend and protect those liberties given to me at birth. Without being faithful to those who serve and protect us, we dishonor those who have died upholding these two documents. Losing that faith in our legacy leaves us vulnerable to tyranny, oppression and future threats of terrorism on our soil.

The Journey is not over because as long as I live, the gifts you have given me will be written in a form that helps to remind